Dressing with Style

A Woman's Guide to Organizing Your Wardrobe and Shopping in Houston

Tina Fondren

SPECTRUM 1993

Copyright © 1993 by Tina Fondren

All rights reserved under International Copyright Law. Published in the United States of America by Spectrum Publishing, Box 571562, Houston, Texas 77257-1562. Contents and/or cover may not be reproduced in whole or in part in any form without the express written consent of the Publisher.

Manufactured in the United States of America.

Excerpts from *A RETURN TO LOVE* Copyright © by Marianne Williamson. Reprinted with permission of Harper Collins Publishers, Inc., 10 East 53rd St., New York, N.Y. 10022.

Excerpts from the *DAILY WORD* Copyright © 1992. Reprinted by permission of Silent Unity's Magazine.

Dressing with Style, A Woman's
Guide to Organizing Your Wardrobe
and Shopping in Houston
ISBN 0-9636352-0-4 $14.95

Tina Fondren
Fashion and Design Consultant
5251 Westheimer, Suite 320
Houston, Texas 77056-1562
(713) 974-0370

Typesetting and design by Brent Comiskey (713) 974-0370 and Michael W. Manuel (713) 953-0650

Contents

I	Thoughts on Fashion and Style: An Introduction	9
II	Retail Stores and Catalog Shopping	15
	Department Stores	16
	Boutiques	17
	Trunk Shows	17
	Catalog Shopping	18
III	Where to Begin	23
	Figure Types	24
	Colors	26
	Fabrics	27
	Fashion Magazines	28
IV	Designers	31
	American, French, Italian, British, Japanese and German Designers	31
	Designer Size Chart	37
	Secondary Lines	37
	Private Label Lines	40
V	Investment Dressing	41
	The Golden Rules of Effective Shopping	42
	Cost Per Wearing	43
VI	Dressing Well for Less	45
	Sale Shopping	45
	Garment Codes	47
	Houston Sale Calendar	48
	How to Make Less Look Like More	49
	Vintage Clothing Stores	50

VII	Wardrobe Building for Women	53
	The Foundation of a Woman's Wardrobe	54
	A Travel Wardrobe	57
	Evening Dressing	60
	What is Your Fashion Signature?	63
	Accessories: The Details That Matter	65
	Fashion Confidence From the French	67
VIII	A Bridal Wardrobe Guide	69
	Finding the Gown of Your Dreams	70
	Houston Bridal Stores	72
	Mothers of the Bride and Groom	74
	Bridesmaids Wardrobe Choices	74
	Wardrobe Planning for Parties	75
	The Honeymoon Wardrobe	76
IX	Wardrobe Building for College Girls	77
	The Basics of a College Girl's Wardrobe	77
	Dressing for Sorority Rush	80
X	Closet Organization: From Chaos to Cleanliness	87
	A Step-by-Step Organization Plan	88
	Wardrobe Inventory & Plan	91
	Clothing Care and Maintenance	110
XI	Houston Beauty and Fashion Experts	117
XII	The Best Shopping in Houston: A Retail Directory	121
Glossary		141
Index		144

Dedicated to the memory of my
grandfather, Fred M. Bruni,
for all his love.

Acknowledgements

To my husband, Bentley, for his unconditional love and support of this book and everything I do in my life.

To my mother, Patti Bruni, for her love, friendship and encouragement of my career in fashion.

To my brother, Brent, for being the sounding board for my book from beginning to end.

To my grandmother, Anita Bruni, who has set an example for me not only in her strengths of character, but as the epitome of classic style and class.

To all my family, friends and colleagues in the Association of Image Consultants International for their support.

To each of my wonderful clients who I always look forward to working with.

To my illustrator, Colleen Jeanne Sauer, for her beautiful illustrations.

To my editor, Michelle Leigh Smith, for her enthusiasm of this project and her hard work fine tuning my book.

To the many people who let me use their quotes; Lisa Galo, Leslie Schlumberger Garcia, Kay King, Lynn Wyatt, Lisa Moore Turano, Page Parkes, Phyllis Hand, Pati Tierney, Cynthia Christ, Linda Segal, Heidi Schulze, Jackie Griffin, Sarah S. Boyd, Mary Lou Retton and Nancy Dukler, author of *Nancy Dukler's Bridal Book*.

Thank you.

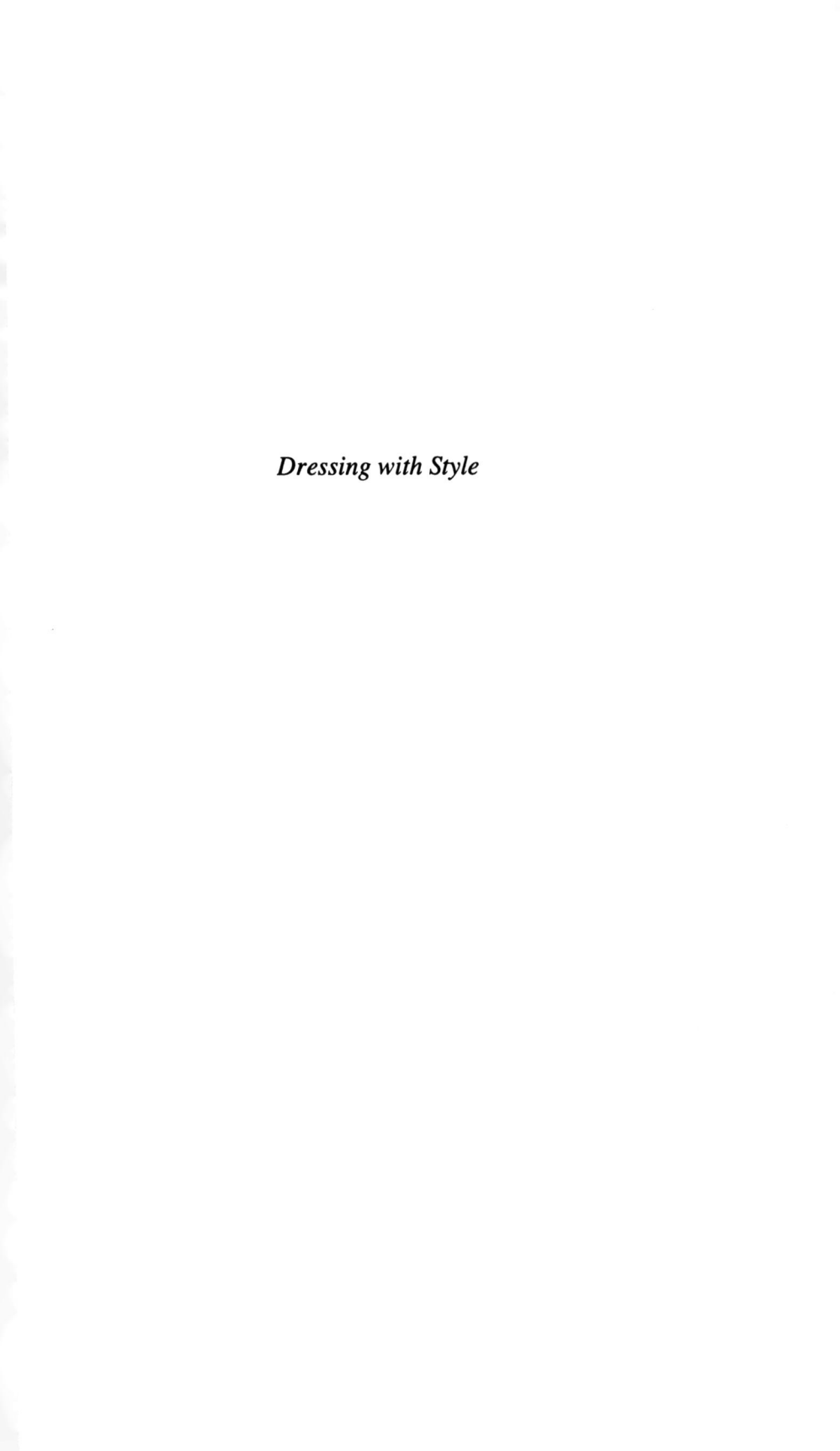

Dressing with Style

I

Thoughts on Fashion and Style: An Introduction

Usually the beginning chapter of a book on fashion does not begin with a personal dialogue from the author but I felt it was important to share with you my feelings on why I wrote this book and what fashion is to me. Women tend to put so much time, money and effort into what they wear - all I want to do is simplify the process with my knowledge as a fashion consultant and help women feel good about themselves and their appearance. Your wardrobe should not be an all- consuming addiction, but simply a reflection of inner happiness. *Dressing with Style* evolved not as a "fashion bible" on the latest trends but as a guide to share with you some basic principles and knowledge I have learned in my years in the fashion industry, to help make your life a little easier, a little less stressful, and little more beautiful.

With the increased cost of living today, more and more women are budgeting what they spend on clothes. Now that the extravagant 80's have been replaced with the recycling 90's, women have other priorities to spend their money on. Public attitude and personal self-perception is saying that conspicuous spending is no longer acceptable in this society. Today it is prestigious to appear the sophisticated and clever shopper. The 90's perspective on shopping is getting the best quality garment, in the quickest amount of time, for the least amount of money. The dilemma is women want to spend less on their appearance but still want to look their best. Who would of thought ten years ago people would actually pay money to have someone come into the privacy of their own home to organize their closet and then do their clothing shopping. Faith Popcorn, author of *The Popcorn Report,* sums up the consumer of the 90's when she stated in her book that personal service, quality merchandise, and stress free purchasing is what the consumer of the 90's not only wants but is getting.

Everyone knows your appearance is not and will never be the most important part of you. What I feel, as I'm sure most people agree, it is your God given inner beauty that is the most important. Even fashion designer Giorgio Armani has stated, "A classic beauty is someone who transcends fashion and outward decoration. Her beauty is innate."

Much research has surfaced especially in the last couple of years about how people perceive you, as well as how you feel about yourself according to how you look. When you feel good about yourself and your appearance, you transpire that positive attitude to the people you interact with. A dear friend gave me a wonderful book, *A Return To Love* by Marianne Williamson. In it she refers to make-up and clothing; "Their point is not to seduce another person, but to add light to the world in the form of beauty and pleasure. The meaning in things is how much we use them to contribute happiness to the world. Clothes and other personal effects are no different than any other art form. If we perceive them lovingly, they can lift the vibrations and increase the energy in the world around us." I feel clothing should not be used to flaunt wealth or intimidate other people but simply add to our positive self image and happiness.

I would also like to share with you some thoughts from the *Daily Word* (a daily inspirational booklet) on appearance. "We may spend a little or a lot of time thinking about, selecting, or preparing the right clothes for an occasion - whether formal, informal, or somewhere in between. What we choose to wear makes a statement about us. Do we also choose the right expression of face, stance of posture, and positiveness of attitude that can make a statement about the inner quality of our thoughts? No matter how casual or appropriate our clothes may be, we can not feel comfortable if we are tense. No matter how much care we give to appearance, we cannot feel joyful if we wear a frown. Our appearance is an outer expression of our positive attitudes and thoughts. These qualities are not things we put on each day, but a free and natural expression of our inner spiritual nature." The truth of the matter is you must be happy from within to have a beautiful appearance because no matter how expensive or beautiful a suit is, it will not mask a frown.

You want people to notice you and what you have to say; not make judgements about you by critiquing your clothing. The advice of the legendary Coco Chanel still holds true today, "Dress shabbily, they notice the dress; dress impeccably, they notice the woman." First impressions make a difference because immediately people make instant judgements about your personality, morals, intelligence, background and job. Especially as women strive to climb the corporate ladder, their image in the workplace becomes increasingly important.

One point I want to clarify is, I am not a proponent of excessive shopping by telling my clients they need to spend thousands of dollars on clothes in order to look their best. Instead, I save my clients time and money by teaching them how to organize their wardrobe, where to invest their clothing budget, and how to utilize their present wardrobe. A client of mine, Jackie Griffin, tells people, "I couldn't afford not to hire Tina." Women today just do not have the time to spend every morning dwelling over what to wear. They want to get dressed quickly, yet still look polished and pulled together. Women want comfort first in their clothing and they want to be able to not worry about what they wearing all day.

In the book I make several references to the style of French women because they always appear to have confidence about themselves and the way they dress. They review the trends and make the look their own by following the theory of Paris shoe designer Robert Clergerie, "More important than fashion is style." I completely agree with him and hopefully, with the information on wardrobe organization and style in *Dressing with Style*, you will be able to develop your own. In the beginning of each of the upcoming chapters are quotes by several Houstonians with great style on what they think style is.

THOUGHTS ON FASHION AND STYLE

I hope you will learn how to organize and utilize your present wardrobe by following the guidelines in *Dressing with Style* and use it as a guide to keep in your purse while shopping.

Very truly yours,

Tina Fondren

Tina Fondren

II

 *Retail Stores and Catalog Shopping*

"Style is a combination of creativity, personal expression, and above all, confidence. If you are a confident self assured woman - you will wear everything well."

-Leslie Schlumberger Garcia
Schlumberger Art &
Design Services, Inc.
President

In order to build upon and maintain a wardrobe you must develop a relationship with one salesperson at each of your favorite stores. Many women are intimidated to walk into high-priced stores or just plain overwhelmed by the vast amount of clothing displayed in stores. Also, they may feel they cannot afford designer clothes or feel the sales people are snobbish. Be open to shopping at new stores because designer merchandise can be affordable when bought on sale. You can learn how to emulate designer looks by looking around, choosing what looks good on you and incorporating the best choices in your own wardrobe.

Department Stores

One of the reasons to shop department stores is they always keep their customers well informed through sales, catalogs, trunk shows and designer personal appearances. In order to receive this information through the mail, you must be a store credit card holder or read the fashion section of the newspaper.

The sales are one of the best reasons to shop at department stores. Department stores deal with an immense amount of merchandise; therefore, they are always the first to begin markdowns. Store credit card holders are contacted through the mail on upcoming sales before the information is announced to the public in the newspaper. Another great fact to know about department stores is they will almost always match a markdown price or full price if another store has the same merchandise marked lower.

Due simply to the fact that department stores are so large, many people feel they are impersonal and cater only to the masses without offering any unique merchandise. The best way to utilize the services of a department store is to work with one salesperson in each department. Once you have established a relationship with a salesperson, he or she will keep you informed on upcoming sales and special events. Especially for women who do not have the time or simply do not enjoy shopping, department stores offer one-stop shopping.

Boutiques

Boutiques offer excellent personal service because their salespeople really get to know their client's likes and dislikes. If a certain garment comes in that the salesgirl knows their client needs, the salesperson will put that garment on hold before it evens hits the sales floor. Another reason women prefer boutique shopping is they can drive right up to the store without worrying about crowded parking and malls. One deterrent of boutique shopping is their sales and return policy are not as flexible as those of department stores. It is also hard for them to find you another size or color of a certain garment if they do not have it in stock. But now more than ever before the personal service, unique merchandise and ease of shopping in boutiques has made the boutique the store of the nineties.

An extension of the boutique is the specialty store. One such store is Tootsies, which over the year has expanded from a tiny boutique into a real fashion force in Houston. Their trunk shows, designer personal appearances, huge dressing rooms, charity benefits and knowledgeable sales staff keep their clientele coming back. Specialty stores are definitely the trend of the future because they meet the needs of the consumer by combining the diverse merchandise of a department store with the intimacy of a boutique.

Trunk Shows

Both department stores and boutiques hold trunk shows throughout the year. If you have the time, attend as many trunk shows as possible. A trunk show is planned when the line's representative brings the designer's upcoming collection to a store. The customer is able to try on the garment, which is not usually the correct size, but the representative is able to help you decide on the proper size. Also, the trunk shows give you the opportunity to order sizes or colors the store is not planning to order. For example, a petite woman may order a size 2 and a full-figured woman may order a size 16. It usually takes about two months for the clothes to arrive and if the fit or color is not right, the stores may or may not require you to buy it depending on their policy. Even if you do not plan to order anything from a trunk show, they are a great way to see the upcoming trends. And if you cannot afford designer clothes, you will have a better understanding of upcoming colors and silhouettes to look for in knockoff designers.

Catalog Shopping

All of your wardrobe basics are available in catalogs: a white shirt, jeans, a cashmere jacket - you could never enter another mall again if you didn't want to. By simply adding interesting jewelry and accessories you can now create a designer look without leaving your home.

Today more than ever before, quality merchandise is offered through catalogs. From my own experience with shopping through catalogs, I think only women who are easy to fit, know whats looks good on them and have the patience to deal with the post office should be catalog shoppers.

The Pluses of Catalog Shopping

- Don't have to deal with crowds, long lines, perfume ladies and parking
- It is time efficient
- Can try on the merchandise in the privacy of your home
- They accept returns

The Downside of Catalog Shopping

- Garments don't always fit according to the size ordered
- Color and quality is often not what you expected
- Must deal with the post office to return
- End up losing money on returns because of shipping costs

The Best of Catalog Shopping

Bergdorf Goodman   1-800-662-5455
P.O. Box 5258
FDR Station
New York, New York 10150-5258
- If you cannot make it to New York, this catalog is the next best thing. Their private label line is beautiful and reasonably priced.

Carushka Bodywear   1-800-247-5113
7716 Kester Avenue
Van Nuys, California 91405
- Very California high fashion workout clothing.

DRESSING WITH STYLE

Dance Fashions 404-998-0002
10390 Alpharetta St., Suite A
Roswell, Georgia 30075
- A retail store that sells the activewear line, Eurotard, through mail order.

Dance France 1-800-421-1543
2503 Main Street
Santa Monica, California 90405
- Dance France carries quality workout clothing basics in bright colors.

Eddie Bauer 1-800-426-8020
Fifth & Union
P.O. Box 3700
Seattle, Washington 98124-3700
- Down-to-earth clothes and outerwear for the outdoors.

Hermes 1-800-441-4488 (ext. 4279)
Monde D' Hermes Department
745 Fifth Avenue, Suite 800
New York, New York 10151-0123
- Hermes is a Parisian tradition carrying luxurious equestrian inspired leather goods and clothing.

James Reid LTD 1-800-545-2056
114 East Palace Avenue
Sante Fe, New Mexico 87501
- James Reid carries absolutely gorgeous Southwestern sterling silver and 14 kt. gold buckles and concho belts.

RETAIL STORES AND CATALOG SHOPPING

J. Crew 1-800-782-8244
One Ivey Crescent
Lynchburg, Virginia 24506-1001
- Everybody loves J.Crew because they carry clothing basics with style at reasonable prices.

J. Peterman Company 1-800-231-7341
P.O. Box 55903
Lexington, Kentucky 4055-9979
- An illustrated catalog carrying hard to find classics such as an Irish hacking jacket, a U.S. navy peacoat and European elk boots.

Many Goats 1-800-937-8920
4500 N. Oracle #433
Tucson, Arizona 85705
- Many Goats' exquisitely illustrated catalog features handcrafted jewelry and belts created by some of the finest Native American artisans on the reservation.

Max Lang 960-8845
Highland Village
4020 Westheimer
Houston, Texas 77027
- Max Lang's beautiful exotic belts and sterling silver buckles are available through his catalog.

Neiman Marcus 1-800-825-8000
Mail Order Division, P.O. Box 2968
Dallas, Texas 75221-2968
- Neiman Marcus sends out a great selection of catalogs

throughout the year- their Christmas one is the best.

Tweeds 1-800-999-7997
1 Avery Row
Roanoke, Virginia 234012
- Tweeds offers great basics similar in feel to J. Crew.

Victoria's Secret 1-800-888-1500
P.O. Box 16589
Columbus, Ohio 43216
- Many Houstonians now receive the Victoria's Secret catalog and the reason for it's success is that their lingerie is very well priced for the quality and style.

Wathne 1-800-942-1166
1095 Cranbury So. River Rd., Suite 8
Jamesburg, New Jersey 08831
- A gorgeous catalog carrying clothing and accessories similar in feel to Hermes and Ralph Lauren.

III

Where to Begin

"Style is both a projected and perceived entity. The personal style one projects may or may not be perceived as intended. What is the personal style of the 'me' that you see? It is your assessment of my uniqueness in visual image, attitude, interaction and performance. If this projection of my individual style is powerful enough, you will perceive my style as I preferred, whether that style is natural or intended."

-KAY KING
HOUSTON COMMUNITY COLLEGE
FASHION DEPARTMENT HEAD

Figure Types

"Clothes should provide the background for a person, not the other way around."

-Calvin Klein

Your figure type directly affects the colors, patterns, fabrics and clothing silhouettes you should wear. The primary reason women purchase unflattering clothing is not knowing their figure type. Every woman has some beautiful feature which makes her unique, but the trick to always looking great is to play up those features with complimenting colors, silhouettes and accessories. When your overall image appears pulled together, people will notice you rather than your figure flaws.

By following the basic silhouettes of these figure types, you can make the most of your body shape.

Petite Figure

Shop for:
- Lightly padded shoulders
- Slim skirts
- Fitted jackets
- Jackets and skirts in monochromatic color
- Dark skirts and slim pants
- Vertical stripes

Avoid:
- Wide legged or cuffed pants
- Bulky gathers at the waist
- Large patterns
- Frilly styles
- Full skirts
- Oversized details like dolman sleeves

WHERE TO BEGIN

Pear Figure

Shop for:
- Strong shoulder lines
- Dark toned skirts and pants
- Below the hip tops
- Moderate to narrow pants
- Long, softly shaped jackets
- Slim skirts

Avoid:
- Tight or clingy jersies and knits
- Poufs or tiered skirts
- Full pants
- Cropped jackets
- Pleated full skirts
- Large patterns on skirts or pants

Boyish Figure

Shop for:
- Jackets with curved shape at the waist
- Peplum jackets
- Wrap blouses and jackets
- All over shirring
- Sarong skirts
- Pleats
- Wide belts

Avoid:
- Boxy jackets
- Droopy shoulders
- Tunics
- Clingy fabrics
- Skimpy camisoles

Full Figure

Shop for:
- Strong shoulders
- Dark colors
- Below the hip tops
- Hose matched to skirt and shoes
- Simple lines

Avoid:
- Strapless, halter or spaghetti straps
- Oversized shapeless clothes
- Tight clothing
- Poufs or tiers
- Wide pants
- Double-breasted jackets
- Sarong skirts

I want to emphasize that these guidelines are not set in stone, but merely a way for you to simplify your shopping. In addition to your figure type, the color, cut, pattern and fabric content should help determine what looks best on you. Remember, the less you take into the dressing room, the less you try on, the quicker you will find what you are looking for.

Colors

By observing and feeling designer Donna Karan's collections, one can see how important color and fabric is to her. Donna thinks black is the perfect color because it always looks expensive. She knows one of the first things a person notices about you are the colors you are wearing. The color of your clothing affects the way you feel about yourself as well as the way people perceive you.

Therefore, it is important to wear colors which flatter your figure and coloring, not compete with them. Certain colors compliment you because of many factors including skin tone, hair color, eye color, height and weight, lighting and even mood and personal perceptions. Always wear the colors you feel the most comfortable in and not because they are the "hot" colors of the season. Usually the colors you feel good in are the ones which look the best.

Fabrics

Most people buy clothing according to color and fit only, and forget to examine the quality of the fabric. First even before color, you should analyze the garment's fabric content. The fabric content will help you to determine whether the purchase is an economical one. The key factors to consider are your budget, the climate you live in and your lifestyle. By investing in top quality fabrics, your clothing will hold up to daily wear and tear.

I recommend Houston women purchase the majority of their clothing in fabrics which do not easily wrinkle, stain or loose their shape. Light weight wools and wool/cotton or wool/silk blends work the best for year-round dressing. All of the jackets and trousers in Donna Karan's collections are made of such fine wool crepe that she says, "You can sleep in it and still look terrific." Wool is static resistant, breathes well, wrinkle resistant and less likely to stain than other fabrics. It breathes naturally in warm weather, yet provides warmth on cool days. The initial cost may be higher but the longer life and luxurious look and feel of the garment is well worth the investment. Also, when purchasing casual cotton clothes, look for cotton blended with a small amount of lycra, which will help it to keep it's shape. Although cotton/

polyester blends cost less, they begin to pill immediately after being washed.

Fashion Magazines

If you are truly interested in maintaining your wardrobe you should invest in a few fashion magazines. Many women only buy magazines which they think are conducive to their age, lifestyle and budget. They should look at others to see upcoming trends and silhouettes. Magazine editorials will begin to open your eyes to new wardrobe combinations and may even entice you to wear something in your wardrobe you have not been wearing. By reading current magazines you can, for the price of the subscription, get ideas for mixing and matching within your current wardrobe and begin a file of silhouettes, colors, fabrics and styles you like. Tear out pages of interest and keep them with you so that when shopping you will have the pages handy.

Allure is one of the newest magazines on the market catering to women of all ages. Their witty articles are interesting and fun to read. They always list the latest in beauty and fashion trends and where they can be found.

Bazaar always prints articles on the arts and politics. Their fashion editorials are sleek and sophisticated and cater to that type of reader.

Elle focuses on interesting fashion editorials because they mix expensive with inexpensive designers to create new and innovative looks.

Vogue magazine is a classic. They show fabulous fashion editorials and always profile interesting celebrities. Women are often intimidated by the high price clothing they show but they now even have a Dress for Less section.

W is a monthly over-sized magazine. They cover the American and European designer collections every season, the international charity and social circuit and beautiful homes all over the world.

Women's Wear Daily like W, is a John Fairchild publication. WWD is a daily trade newspaper read mostly by those in the fashion industry and cannot be bought at stores. It profiles industry stocks, new retail developments and designer collections. It is a valuable tool to anyone in the fashion industry.

Houston Post and Houston Chronicle Fashion Sections which come out in the Thursday editions always list the Houston designer trunk shows and personal appearances in their fashion calendar. They cover local retail and social news as well as the American and European collections.

Style with Elsa Klensch is a weekly 30-minute television program on CNN which airs on Saturdays at 9:30 A.M. and 1:30 P.M. Hosted by Elsa Klensch, the program profiles designers, models, and interior decorators and covers the fashion highlights in collections from all over the world.

* To order magazines at up to 70% off retail prices, call Abe Greenberg Magazines at 1-800-457-3443.

IV

Designers

"Clothes are only a part of one's life. Style is the way one lives that life. I feel my style comes more from the feeling I have inside- femininity, confidence, strength and sense of humor. One's image is only partly established by one's style. But your character is you - you in the dark. Character is not something you develop in a crisis; it's what you exhibit in a crisis...you had it all the time. That's style."

— LYNN WYATT

American Designers

Joseph Abboud
Linda Allard for Ellen Tracy
Mark Badgley and James Mischka for Badgley Mischka
Geoffrey Beene
Bill Blass

Barry Bricken
Liz Claiborne
Oscar de la Renta
Louis Dell' Olio
Pamela Dennis
Kathryn Dianos
Mark Eisen
Byron Lars
Steve Fabrikant
Jennifer George
James Galanos
Gordon Henderson
Carolina Herrera
Isani
Betsey Johnson
Andrea Jovine
Gemma Kahng
Norma Kamali
Donna Karan
Jeanette Kastenberg
Calvin Klein
Michael Kors
Ralph Lauren
Liancarlo
Bob Mackie
Mary McFadden
Nicole Miller
Nolan Miller
Isaac Mizrahi
Debra Moises
Josie Natori
Christian Frances Roth
Fernando Sanchez
Arnold Scassi
Anna Sui
Zang Toi
Isabel Toledo
Susie Tompkins of Esprit

DESIGNERS

Richard Tyler for Anne Klein
Joan Vass
Adrienne Vittadini
Emily Cinader Woods of J. Crew
Zoran

French Designers

Agnes De Fleurieu of Agnes B
Azzedine Alaia
Balenciaga
Pierre Balmain
Barbara Bui
Jean-Charles de Castelbajac
Celine
Karl Lagerfeld for Chloe
Christian Dior
Pierre Cardin
Karl Lagerfeld for Chanel
Courreges
Karl Lagerfeld
Herve Leger
Oscar de la Renta for Pierre Balmain
Jacqueline de Ribes
Jaques Fath
Louis Feraud
Jean- Paul Gaultier
Hubert De Givenchy
Madame Gres
Hermes
Emmanuelle Khanh
Christian Lacroix

33

Lanvin
Ted Lapidus
Guy Laroche
Leonard
Claude Montana
Thierry Mugler
Bernard Perris
Myrene de Premonville
Paco Rabanne
Nina Rici
Sonia Rykiel
Helmut Lang
Yves Saint Laurent
Jean- Louis Scherrer
Martine Sitbon
Angelo Tarlazzi
Chantel Tomass
Emanuel Ungaro

Italian Designers

Giorgio Armani
Laura Biagiotti
Byblos
Ernestina Cerini
Cerruti
Complice
Domenico Dolce and Stefano Gabbana for Dolce & Gabbana
Donatella Girombelli for Genny
Gucci
Fendi

Salvatore Ferragamo
Gianfranco Ferre
Alberta Ferretti
Romeo Gigli
Mariuccia Mandelli for Krizia
Max Mara
Enrica Massei
Rosita Missoni for Missoni
Anna Molinari
Franco Moschino
Miuccia Prada for Prada
Emilio Pucci
Mila Schon
Giorgio di Sant Angelo
Valentino
Gianni Versace

British Designers

John Galliano
Katherine Hammnett
Bruce Oldfield
Rifat Ozbek
Jean Muir
Zandra Rhodes
Vivienne Westwood

Japanese Designers

Kenzo
Rei Kawakubo for Comme des Garcons
Matsuda
Issey Miyake
Hanae Mori
Yuki Torii
Yohji Yamamoto

German Designers

Natalie Acatrini
Escada
Wolfgang Joop
Mondi
Jill Sander

The designers and fashion houses listed above are not always from the country or produce their fashion shows in the country they design in. Also, this list only includes the most established clothing designers and excludes designers who only produce accessories.

Once you know your body type and know which designers fit you the best, shopping will become easier and far less frustrating. The following chart is a size equivalent breakdown according to country.

Designer Size Chart

U.S.A.	4	6	8	10	12	14
France	34	36	38	40	42	44
Great Britain	6	8	10	12	14	16
Italy	38	40	42	44	46	48
Japan	small	small	med.	med.	large	large
Germany	34	36	38	40	42	44

Secondary Lines

Designers are finally meeting the needs of consumers by giving them style at affordable prices with secondary collections, also called diffusion lines. Secondary lines offer clothes with style at reasonable prices. Anna Wintour, the editor of "Vogue" stated, "Designers have definitely responded to the economic situation by expanding to the secondary market." Every top designer is producing a diffusion line or at least is in the process of it, which means that women can now afford to look fashionable without getting a second mortgage on their home.

Women in the 80's wore the same designer label from head to toe, but the woman of the 90's wears a more creative, individualistic look. Even the women who can afford to pay couture prices are listening to their conscience and buying the more economically priced secondary lines.

Many Houston stores already carry a wide range of secondary lines. Sara Boyd, owner of the boutique Ms., favors secondary lines because they give her customers "the essence of the designer without designer price tags." In addition to clothing, many of the secondary lines include handbags, shoes and costume jewelry.

The next time you are out shopping, keep secondary lines in mind. They will enable you to wear a designer look without breaking your budget.

SIGNATURE LINE	SECONDARY LINE
Giorgio Armani	Emporio Armani
	A/X Armani
Geoffery Beene	Mr. Beene
Bill Blass	Blassport
Byblos	Options by Byblos
	Vis a Vis by Byblos
	Byblos Blu
Escada	Laurel
	Crisca
	Apriori
Fendi	Fendi 365
	Fendissime
John Galliano	Galliano's Girl
John Paul Gaultier	Junior Gaultier
Gianfranco Ferre	Studio 000.1 by Ferre
	Oaks
Romeo Gigli	G. Gigli
Katherine Hamnett	Katherine Hamnett Active
Carolina Herrera	CH Carolina Herrera
Isani	Isani Studio
	Isani Shirts
Norma Kamali	Norma Kamali Basics
	1-800-8-Kamali
Donna Karan	Donna Karan Essentials
	DKNY
	DKNY Jeans
Anne Klein	Anne Klein II
	A Line

DESIGNERS

Calvin Klein Collection...	CK Calvin Klein
	Calvin Klein Jeans
Michael Kors...	Kors
Krizia...	Krizia Poi
	MM by Krizia
	KM by Krizia
	K by Krizia
	Krizia Maglia
Karl Lagerfeld...	KL by Lagerfeld
Ralph Lauren...	Ralph Lauren Classics
	Ralph Lauren Activewear
	Ralph Lauren Country
Leonard...	Leonard I.D.
Bob Mackie...	Bob Mackie Collection II
Issey Miyake...	Plantation by Miyake
Claude Montana...	The State of Montana
Moschino...	Moschino Cheap and Chic
	Moschino Jeans
Thierry Mugler...	Thierry Mugler Active
Jean Muir...	Jean Muir Studio
Rifat Ozbek...	Future Ozbek
	O for Ozbek
Prada...	Miu Miu
Emanuel Ungaro Parallel..	Ungaro Solo Donna
	Emanuel
Oscar de la Renta...	Oscar de la Renta Studio
Valentino...	Miss V
	Oliver
Joan Vass...	Joan Vass, U.S.A.
Gianni Versace...	Istante
	Versus
Yves Saint Laurent...	Rive Gauche
	YSL Encore
Zang Toi...	Z

Private Label Lines

- A private label is a line of clothing or accessories a store produces in the states or abroad which is sold exclusively at that store.

- The line is usually named after the store or may have a designer name.

- The line represents the style of the store. A store may only sell their private label line or they may sell it in addition to other designer labels.

- Private label lines offer the season's best looks at lower than designer prices.

Store	Private Label Line
Ann Taylor	Ann Taylor Studio
Marshall Field's	Charter Club
Barneys	Barneys New York Private Collection
Episode	Episode
Saks Fifth Avenue	The Works
Tootsies	Tootsies
Vikki	Vikki

V

Investment Dressing

"Style is both taste and class. Style is poise and confidence. Put those together with a sense of what looks good on your body and what fits your lifestyle, and that is dressing with style."

- LISA MOORE TURANO
OF COUNCIL ENTERPRISES, INC.
PRESIDENT

"I have a closet full of clothes and nothing to wear!" This is a fairly common complaint of many American women, but it is primarily because they do not know how to shop. Women don't need to be frustrated every time they go into their closet. To help women conquer this dilemma, I teach them the principles of shopping used by French women. French women always appear elegant, chic and confident. Their sense of style can be learned by following a few simple shopping guidelines.

The Golden Rules of Effective Shopping

- Never shop for an outfit the day of an event which is like going grocery shopping when your are starving - you will buy anything.

- If you are feeling glum don't try to cure your blues by shopping but go exercise your body, not your credit card.

- No matter how low an item is marked down, it is not a bargain if you are never going to wear it.

- Bad shopping habits will only get you into debt or give you a closet full of nothing.

The number one mistake women make when shopping is buying poor quality garments. The theory of investment dressing states it is better to buy a few good quality clothes than than have a closet overflowing with a ton of low quality clothing; basically, think quality, not quantity. From a consumer point of view, it is far more cost effective to spend your clothing budget on top quality clothing. If you buy a high quality designer blazer you can wear it for many years. Not only will the fabric last, the cut will withstand the trends.

Cost Per Wearing

"Black is the foundation of all good wardrobes."
Parisian fashion designer, Karl Lagerfeld

The way to figure out if you are following the rules of investment dressing is to calculate the Cost Per Wearing before purchasing a garment or accessory. In order to figure the Cost Per Wearing, take the price of the item and divide it by the number of times it will probably be worn. If you were to purchase a black and white Hermes scarf for $200 and wear it once a week for eight years, the C.P.W. would be only .48 cents a wearing. And an Hermes scarf will last much longer than eight years. Or if you purchase a classic Calvin Klein light weight wool blazer, you can wear it year-round with skirts, pants or jeans. If the blazer cost $600, and you wore it three times a month for five years, the C.P.W. would be $3.30. While $600 may seem high for one garment, not only will the quality and cut of the garment stand the test of time, you will look and feel more polished.

What exactly is investment dressing? The investment theory is buying a few high quality clothes rather than buying more and more clothes just to fill a closet bulging with low quality garments. Mirella Petteni Haggiag, who is known as one of the most stylish women in Rome, thinks most women's wardrobes, "are overloaded; too many choices only creates self-doubt. I want to simplify my life, not waste time trying to decide what to wear." An obvious proponent of the investment theory of dressing she says, " I buy things that will stay with me forever and depending on my mood, I change accessories." Chapter VII lists the classic clothing which will last you through years of changing trends.

Invest in the classics first, but also know when to splurge and when to scrimp. When shopping look for seasonless clothing, clothes that can go from day into evening. Most women make the mistake of spending too much on fads. Many seasons ago the big trend was Pucci print dresses and leggings. Instead buying the dress, buy the matching headband, then get rid of it next season without guilt. Trendy items are a great way to update your wardrobe but you should look for designer copies or buy these items on sale.

Investment dressing begins with a shift in thinking and with a little practice, you can turn a closet full of nothing to wear into a wardrobe overflowing with style. So next time you are about to purchase a piece of clothing or accessory, ask yourself the following questions.

- Is the fabric high quality?

- Is the fabric year round or seasonal for my climate?

- Do the details such as the lining, buttons and seams look high quality?

- Will it mix and match with at least five other pieces in my wardrobe?

- Does the color compliment my hair and skin color?

- Is this garment classic or trendy?

- What is the Cost Per Wearing of this garment?

VI

Dressing Well for Less

"Style is dressing to project an image of someone comfortable with themself. I find the more we are able to be ourselves, the more acceptance we receive from others. In this manner, we are able to assume an image of professionalism at the same time."

> *- PAGE PARKES*
> *PAGE PARKES CENTER OF*
> *MODELING AND INTERMEDIA*
> *MODELING AGENCY*
> *PRESIDENT*

Sale Shopping

If you have the eye for Armani, but a budget for the Gap, sale shopping is the solution. Forget your grandmother's adage, "never buy anything on sale that you wouldn't pay full price for." Your grandmother didn't have Neiman Marcus Last Call.

Why Sale Shopping Makes Sense Today

- Stores receive their merchandise so early in the season that by the time you are ready to wear them, the clothes are already on sale.

- The early sales in department stores force competing boutiques to start their sales.

- Many designer garments are classic in cut and are made of year-round fabrics which enable you to wear last season's merchandise this year and for many years to come.

Strategies for Successful Shopping

- Visit stores regularly.
- Get to know salespeople.
- Ask stores to match their competitor's markdowns.
- Never wait until the last minute to purchase special occasion pieces.
- Shop with the next season in mind.
- Know how many alterations will be necessary.
- Get on mailing lists by applying for store credit cards and signing up on boutique mailing lists.
- Check fashion section of the newspaper for sale ads.
- Be aware of return policies in case your purchase does not mix and match with your wardrobe.
- Shop sales.
- Shop in comfortable shoes and clothes that are not a production to take off and put back on.
- Never shop on the spur of the moment, instead, always have a plan of action that includes a list of stores, addresses

and items needed.
- Plan your store route ahead of time in order to save time and gas.
- Keep a wish list on hand of wardrobe needs and wants.

What to Buy on Sale

- Trendy clothes you would not pay full price for.
- Classics such as the little black dress, a cashmere sweater, loafers, a great navy jacket or black satin evening shoes.
- Fill in pieces for your wardrobe.

* It is best to buy designer clothes on sale because of the quality and better fit of the clothes. Casual, inexpensive clothes can always be bought at full price.

The Price Life of a Designer Jacket

Day one - $ 900
After three months - $ 630 (30% off)
After four and a half months - $ 450 (50% off)
After six months - $270 (70% off)

Garment Codes

When shopping in discount stores which remove designer labels, you can still identify the RN or WPL number listed on the care label. The codes of the most established designers are as follows:

- Geoffrey Beene - RN 33293, RN 64885
- Eleanor P. Brenner - RN 38746
- Liz Claiborne - RN 5002
- Oscar de la Renta - RN 54563, RN50032
- Dior - WPL 07074, RN 03005
- Perry Ellis - RN 57272
- Jones New York - RN 54050, RN 54897
- Donna Karan - RN 68596
- Anne Klein - RN 77464, RN 40803, RN 75572
- Calvin Klein - RN 41327, RN 42642, RN 64754
- Karl Lagerfeld - RN 67634
- Ralph Lauren - RN 67635
- Nolan Miller - RN 77730, RN 78717
- Evan- Picone - RN 35685, WPL 08582
- St. Gillian - RN 47313

Houston Sale Calendar

Jan. 1	Famous Semi-Annual Sale - Talbot's
Jan. 2	Designer Dress Sale - Saks Fifth Avenue
Jan. 16	Last Call - Neiman Marcus
Jan.	Winter Sale - The Cotton Club
Feb. 14	50% to 75% Off Coat Sale - Neiman Marcus
Mar. 16	St. Patrick's Day Sale - The Cotton Club
Apr. 1	April Fool's Day Sale - The Cotton Club
Jun.	Summer Sale - The Cotton Club
Jul. 23	Last Call - Neiman Marcus
Nov. 23	Post Thanksgiving Sale - Saks Fifth Avenue

* The above sale calendar is just a sample of the many sales throughout the year in Houston.

How to Make Less Look Like More

With a bit of ingenuity and careful shopping, it is possible to dress with style while on a budget. A little can go a long way by following a few simple guidelines.

- For designer clothes and accessories, sales held in January and July have the lowest prices. Even though many people believe Neiman Marcus prices are beyond their budget, every Last Call (their bi-annual big sale), the store sells designer clothes up to 70% off.

- Visit Houston's resale and vintage shops for interesting clothing and accessories.

- Academy is a great place to buy Hanes white T-shirts and socks.

- Check out the boy's and men's department for oxford cloth shirts, sweaters, pocket squares, jean jackets and raincoats.

- Don't forget the pre-teen or junior department for petite women.

- Buy camisoles, bustiers and leggings in the lingerie department.

- Look for bodysuits, slippers, shorts, leggings and shorts at dance and exercise wear shops.

- Don't overlook your husband/boyfriend's closet for menswear clothing.

- Riding and hunting stores are a great place to find shirts, belts and riding pants.

- Don't overlook import stores for inexpensive accessories. Pier I carries colorful bracelets, ethnic inspired earrings and great headbands.

Remember to always.......

- Wear properly fitted clothing.
- Wear dark colors - they look more elegant and costly.
- Discard and replace inexpensive, cheaply made belts that often come with clothing.
- Replace inexpensive looking buttons.
- Stitch down or remove protruding pockets.
- Replace overly large shoulder pads for smaller ones.
- Iron faithfully and dry-clean as little as possible.
- Hand wash instead of laundering.
- Stick with the classics.

Vintage Clothing Stores

The following stores offer the best vintage shopping for interesting additions to your wardrobe or costume closet. Items to look for include Levi jeans, antique lace dresses and eclectic accessories. All donations are tax deductible.

Blue Bird Circle Resale Shop   528-0470
615 W. Alabama
Houston, Texas 77006

Cheap Dot's   522-4840
1412 Westheimer
Houston, Texas 77006

The Guild Shop   528-5095
2009 Dunlavy
Houston, Texas 77006

Grandma's Attic   520-1408
1500 W. Alabama
Houston, Texas 77006

Step Back   522-7997
3939 Montrose
Houston, Texas 77006

Timeless Taffeta   529-6299
1657 Westheimer
Houston, Texas 77006

Wear It Again Sam   523-5258
1411 Westheimer
Houston, Texas 77006

VII

Wardrobe Building for Women

> "Style is a signature - something you can create for yourself that becomes 'your own look.' This has no reflection on how much you spend on your clothes or what designer you wear. It is simply a matter of how you put things together to create a look that people will recognize as 'you'."
>
>   - *PHYLLIS HAND*
>   *PHYLLIS HAND PHOTOGRAPHY*
>   *OWNER*

When buying your wardrobe foundation pieces, choose understated neutral colored classics in year round fabrics such as wool crepe or wool gabardine. Spare, well-made clothes always look tasteful and elegant. A closet that possesses the key wardrobe basics is not boring; it simply makes getting dressed easier.

Regardless of age or profession, begin by buying black as your basic wardrobe color. In a recent interview by Mirabella magazine, fashion designer Sonia Rykiel was asked why she always wears black. She answered , "What is important to me is, not so much the clothes I wear. Clothes are just the envelope, and then I use accessories to amuse: necklaces, belts, jeweled or gold handbags, scarves, dangling earrings with a lot of brilliance, and colored shoes- red, green, blue. But always with black." Spoken like a true French woman, Sonia Rykiel understands an essential fashion secret. Black is versatile, compliments all skin tones, and endures season after season. It will also mix well with practically any other color.

No matter how many clothes you have in your closet, if you don't have the key pieces, you will still feel as if you have nothing to wear. Donna Karan says, " A good jacket with a masculine cut is essential. It can go over jeans, black tie, beach clothes." Remember, the key to classic style is quality, not quantity.

The Foundation of a Woman's Wardrobe

Two suits	• Black light weight wool crepe 　- Straight skirt • Gabardine in a neutral color 　- Straight skirt
Three blazers	• Light weight wool or gabardine
Two skirts	• Light weight wool or gabardine
One black dress	• Light weight wool crepe • Simple neckline

WARDROBE BUILDING

Two silk blouses	• Cream silk blouse with collar and French cuffs • Cream silk, round collared blouse
Three sweaters	• One black fitted • One white or cream fitted - mercerized cotton is perfect for year-round • One black cardigan
One pair of pants	• Light weight wool or gabardine • Soft pleats in the front • Leg width-medium
Three pairs of shoes	• Black leather, patent and suede
Three purses	• Leather everyday purse • Evening purse • Totebag
Two belts	• Alligator or lizard belt • Leather belt
Two scarves	• One black and white • One brightly colored
Jewelry	• Pearl necklace • Pearl earrings

Pieces to Mix in for Casual

Shirts	• White Hanes T-shirts • White men's shirt
Skirt	• Fitted black skirt of quality wool or rayon-lycra knit
Pants	• Jeans • Black leggings
Purses and shoes	• Neutral colors such as brown and black
Boots	• Lizard, leather or suede
Belts	• Lizard or alligator with silver buckle • Concho belt
Jewelry	• Eclectic costume

A Travel Wardrobe

Whether you are going to Colorado, the Caribbean or just driving to Galveston for the weekend, you will want to get a lot of style in a little suitcase. "Summer is about simplifying, it's paring down to the essentials, the key pieces that pull you all together," says fashion designer Donna Karan. "In the summer it's very important for clothes to be able to take you from day to evening. That's one reason black and white work so well - it can take you anywhere, and just by adding color as an accent, you can change the feeling." By following her advice for both warm and cool weather vacations and taking chic, streamlined pieces that mix and match you can take off in comfort and style. Remember, clothes that are versatile and not the least bit fussy will give you the easy understated look you want. Besides, who wants to worry about your clothes while on vacation?

Bare Minimum Vacation Basics

- Double-duty tank style bathing suits and leotards
- Sarong skirts
- Simple chemise dress
- Pareos
- Straw hat

- Baseball cap
- Ballet slippers
- Leggings
- White T-shirts
- Bicycle shorts
- Short sleeve ribbed top
- Men's white shirt

Cool Weather Vacation Classics

- Black turtleneck
- Ski parka
- Jean jacket
- Flannel shirt
- Black stirrup pants
- Tweed jacket
- Jeans
- Cowboy boots
- Hiking boots
- Jean shirt
- Cashmere sweater
- Brown loafers
- Bandana or scarf
- Khaki pants

Jet Packing Tips

- Think multi-purpose
- Eliminate the non-essentials
- Never take linen clothing unless you want to spend your vacation ironing
- Pack enough socks and lingerie to last the whole trip

Preparation One Week Before

- Make an activity list to plan your wardrobe
- Try everything on
- Make sure all clothes are clean and in good shape
- Plan one bottom for every two tops
- Everything should be able to be worn at least three ways
- Take only broken in shoes and leave new ones at home

Secrets of Suitcase Packing

- Keep all of your travel essentials at home in one place so you never forget anything, such as a travel alarm, iron or hair dryer
- Arrange a closely packed suitcase to avoid shifting
- Cushion jewelry in tissue to avoid breakage
- Stuff toes of shoes with tissue and wrap with tissue before placing in shoe covers
- Wrap belts and purses in plastic bags and tissue that the dry-cleaning comes in
- Place heavy items at the bottom
- Put all liquids in small plastic bottles
- Put cosmetics and toiletries into zip-lock plastic bags
- Tag suitcases on the inside and out, in case the outer tags fall off
- Place valuables and those can't live-without items in your purse or carry-on luggage
- Don't forget to pack safety pins, scissors, spot remover, a lint brush and Ivory soap

Evening Dressing

"Mixing is the modern way to dress-sporty tops with evening looks or gold jackets with grey flannels."
- Carolina Herrera

Especially during the holiday season you are always invited to at least ten parties and must plan ten fabulous outfits. Instead of worrying all week about what to wear or shopping the day of an event only to resort to buying something that does not fit properly or that you will never wear again, plan ahead.

Evening dressing has changed-instead of puchasing an outfit for a specific occasion, extend your wardrobe by buying separates. Restaurants, gallery openings, parties at friend's houses is about as dressed up as most people get most of the time. Now even at formal events such as charity balls, deb balls and weddings it is considered appropriate to wear cocktail separates and even pants. You feel more comfortable, look great and at the same time are saving money by utilizing your wardrobe to it's maximum potential. This is the nineties way of dressing for the evening. The possibilities are endless - with an open mind and a litttle creativity. The key is to stay open to new proportions and combinations. There are no rules.

Factors to consider before making any purchases are: the time of day of the party, if it is a professional or personal atmosphere, the type of party, and what you already have in your wardrobe. First, pull all of your evening clothing, shoes and accessories out of your closet to better evaluate your options. Bring out clothing you may have never thought of as "evening dress" but might work.

Try on everything and experiment with mixing and matching. Then make a pile of alterations, give aways, possible outfits and clothes that need matching pieces. Make a list of all possible outfits, items to look for, and unmatched pieces in a separate bag which will serve as a guide. It is important to take unmatched pieces with you while shopping to make sure the colors and shapes match. This process will not only save you time and money in the long run, but much frustration deciding what to wear before each party.

Evening Classics

Metallics	• Gold and silver sweaters, leathers, shoes and purses
Velvet and Velour	• Pants, leggings, jeans, skirts and dresses
Color	• Black, winter white, red, cream, navy, deep browns, hunter green, gold and silver
Bustiers	• Under blazers in lace or beaded fabrics
Jackets	• Tuxedo styles
Shirts	• A white or cream silk or organza blouse with French cuffs. Tuxedo shirts

DRESSING WITH STYLE

Sweaters	• Cashmere, sweater sets, black turtlenecks, fitted body suits
Pants	• Velvet, tuxedo pants, velour leggings
Skirts	• Fitted and long, full and long, fitted and short, full and short
Dresses	• The slip dress, the little black dress, a column dress
Coats	• Furs are out, evening trench coats, black wool coats, evening wraps
Shoes	• Strappy pumps, velvet slippers
Hose	• Black, nude, shine, lace
Fabrics	• Sheer, chiffon, silk, lace, velvet, velour
Jewelry	• Pearls, interesting costume jewelry

The Little Black Dress

"Elegance in clothes means being able to move freely. These dresses that won't pack into airplane luggage .....ridiculous!"

*Coco Chanel -
The original designer
of the L.B.D.*

The L.B.D. is.....

- The cornerstone of any woman's wardrobe
- Always flattering, elegant and sophisticated
- Never dated
- Always appropriate anytime and anywhere
- Unlimited in the number of looks by adding jackets, jewelry and scarves

What is Your Fashion Signature?

Your fashion signature is the detail that says "It's me." Whether you are in finance, fashion, or education, a signature sets you apart. A trademark should grow out of your personal style and personality. Yves Saint Laurent has said, "All a woman needs is a black sweater, a black skirt, and a man who loves her on her arm." The point being you do not need closets full of clothes to be stylish. Always improvise and experiment, and sometimes go against the rules. The look of the women of the nineties is not a designer look from head to toe or reflective of a specific trend, but indicative of how she as an individual wants to put herself together. Women shouldn't and don't want to be slaves to designers and trends; they want to create their own image. Do not wear the same designer from head to toe but mix different designers together. Just by adding a fabulous pair of earrings or a wonderful print scarf you can give life to a simple black dress. Even fashion designer Gianni Versace advocates individuality in dressing by saying, " Fashion is no longer about day and night. It's about how you feel, what you are, and how you best express yourself." Trends come and go but a fashion signature is a personal stamp that withstands time.

Ways to Cultivate A Fashion Signature

EXAGGERATION. Paloma Picasso's red lips and Liz Claiborne's owl-like eye glasses.

SPONTANEITY. Don't try too hard- fashion should be and appear effortless. Use a scarf as a belt for jeans.

REPETITION. For example, always wearing a hat, pin or big earrings.

CONTRADICTION. Wearing pearls with jeans and cowboy boots or wearing a man's tux shirt and cocktail pants to a black tie event.

COLOR. Nancy Reagan's favorite color to dress in is red. Legendary fashion editor, Diana Vreeland was famous for painting everything from her walls to her lips in Chinese lacquer red.

CONFIDENCE. As long as your attire is appropriate for the occasion don't be concerned about your clothing, just be yourself and you will always look fabulous.

Fashion signature ideas include wearing...

- Your hair pulled back in a chignon or headband
- Wildly colored and patterned socks
- Ten bangle bracelets on one arm
- A certain favorite color
- An interesting pin or two on your blazer lapel
- A scarf either in your hair, or around your neck or waist
- Clothing extremes, such as leather and lace

Accessories: The Details That Matter

"Accessories should be used like exclamation points, to add excitement and energy to an outfit."

– Accessories designer, Gene Meyer, formerly with the house of Geoffrey Beene.

Accessories are the easiest and most economical way to update a wardrobe. If you are tired of your old navy work suit or weekend jeans, purchasing a few key accessories will instantly brighten your wardrobe.

By investing in classic accessories and spending less on trendy items, you will build a timeless, yet diversified wardrobe. Accessories designer Paloma Picasso has known these tricks for years by only wearing simple classic clothing and accenting them

DRESSING WITH STYLE

with her own outstanding accessories. Begin by evaluating your wardrobe and reviewing the fashion magazines for trends, then make a list of key accessories that will make the most of your wardrobe. After you have mastered the art of accessorizing, you will see how easy it is to instantly update clothing and give new clothing a stamp of originality.

* Buy designer knockoffs at chain stores and designer accessories on sale.

Classic Accessories to Invest In

Purses	• High quality leathers can last for years by being re-dyed
Belts	• Thin alligator belt, wide leather belt
Scarves	• Two silk scarves: one black and white and one colored
Jewelry	• Pearl earrings and necklace, a classic watch, ethnic jewelry

Trendy Accessories to Look For

Costume jewelry	• Unique earrings and pins
Hair accessories	• Headbands, barrettes
Casual purses	• Totebags and week-end purses

Sensational Scarves

A scarf, especially ones by Hermes, is a favorite accessory of French women and because most of a French woman's wardrobe consists of solid neutral colors, she will invest in many brightly colored scarves. Favorite scarf patterns include plaids, polka dots, paisleys and stripes.

Whether used as an accent to "dress up" or "casualize" an outfit, a scarf is an eye-catching feminine touch. Think of a scarf as jewelry to play up your clothing.

The Many Ways to Wear A Scarf

- Tied in your hair around a low ponytail
- Wrapped around your head the way Grace Kelly wore hers in *To Catch a Thief*
- Tied on a purse or totebag
- In the belt loops of skirts, pants or jeans
- Around the neck in a multitude of ways
- Tied across a short skirt like a sarong
- In your hair as a headband
- Across your bust as a bustier

Fashion Confidence From the French

Most French women have such style that people believe they are beautiful even if they are not. They know how to flaunt their best features and hide their flaws. Many American women, by contrast, tend to wear what they think looks good on their best friend or their mother.

Learn how to break the fashion rules and make fashion work

for you by mixing traditional with trendy, casual with formal, antique with new and inexpensive with expensive. Don't be afraid to mix designer labels or patterns.

Imagine a French woman strolling down the Champs-Elysees in an Yves Saint Laurent blazer, a freshly pressed men's undershirt, old jeans and lizard cowboy boots. Although each item is contradictory, the combination is fabulous.

VIII

A Bridal Wardrobe Guide

"A personal expression of what you feel inside by using clothing, jewelry, hair styling and make-up expertise. 'ULTIMATE' style is using seasoned professionals to guide you in all of these areas."

> - Cynthia Christ
> Sensia Make-up Studio,
> Sensia Cosmetics
> President and Founder

The months leading up to a wedding can be frustrating and nerve wracking for not just the bride, but for everyone in the wedding. I combined my knowledge as a former bride, bridesmaid and as a fashion consultant to formulate these wardrobe guidelines to make the bride's planning a little easier.

Finding the Gown of Your Dreams

Most wedding dresses are custom ordered to fit the bride's measurements following the manufacturer's size chart. The order must be placed no less than three months before the wedding date. If the bride is a borderline size, the larger size should be ordered because alterations can always be made.

Bridal Gown Choices

If the wedding is formal daytime or formal evening choose a white or ivory floor length wedding dress with a cathedral or chapel length train. The veil should cover the train or extend to the train length. Shoes should match the gown and gloves are optional.

If the wedding is informal daytime or informal evening choose a white, or ivory floor length, tea length or short dress or suit. A short veil or bridal hat and shoes to match will compliment the gown. Gloves are optional.

The Second Wedding Bride

Whether the wedding is informal or formal, an ivory cocktail dress or suit with matching shoes is the appropriate choice. Gloves are optional.

Bridal Designers

VICTOR COSTA. Classic and trendy gowns and suits for brides and bridesmaids. Minimal lace and beading. Moderate price point.

GALINA. For the classic romantic bride. An abundance of lace and beading. High price point.

JIM HJELM. Classic gowns with modern touches. Unique lace and beading. High price point.

SCASSI FOR EVA FORSYTH. Sophisticated dresses often fitted and off the shoulder. Minimal lace and beading. Moderate to high price point.

JESSICA McCLINTOCK. Victorian inspired romantic gowns for brides and bridesmaids in classic styles. Mostly lace and little beading. Lower to moderate price points.

VERA WANG. Gorgeous classic yet different gowns designed by a young talented New York designer. Medium to high price points.

Bridal Wardrobe Checklist

- ( ) Gown
- ( ) Headpiece and Veil
- ( ) Jewelry
- ( ) Bra
- ( ) Gloves
- ( ) Slip / Petticoat
- ( ) Hosiery
- ( ) Garter
- ( ) Shoes

Bridal Fashion Faux Pas

The bride is the star of the wedding, so when all eyes are upon the bride there is no room for fashion victims.

Fashion faux pas to avoid on the wedding day....

- Veils which stand a foot off the bride's head or have a forehead necklace
- Overpowering headpieces
- Helmet head hair
- Oversized rhinestone earrings, necklace or bracelets
- White or glittering hose
- Over-exposed decollete
- Shoes which are metallic and have excessive bows or appliques
- Pastel colored bridal gowns
- Bridal gowns with excessive ruffles

Houston Bridal Stores

Beautiful U   963-8213
3701 West Alabama, Suite 385
Houston, Texas 77027
- Arlene Gamble at Beautiful U custom designs headpieces and bridal veils to your specification.

Bride N' Formal   791-1886
7807 South Main
Houston, Texas 77030
- Bride N' Formal offers Houston's largest selection of bridal gowns and bridesmaids dresses to fit every bridal budget.

In addition, they stock a complete line of headpieces and veils, dyeable matching shoes, mothers' dresses and all neccessary wedding accessories. There are 17 locations in Houston.

Brides 622-2298
2031 Post Oak Blvd.
Houston, Texas 77056
- Brides carries beautiful lines including Galina, Jim Hjelm and Cristos in addition to many services for the bride.

Louise Blum 622-5571
Galleria II
Houston, Texas 77056
- Louise Blum carries absolutely beautiful bridal gowns and their bridesmaid dresses have a more sophisticated look than most. Their services to the bride range from dressers to assist you on your wedding day, custom designed head pieces and bridal gown delivery service.

Mary Ann Maxwell 529-3939
3131 Diamico
Houston, Texas 77019
- Mary Ann Maxwell is a Houston tradition for brides and debutantes. She combines impeccable personal service with an exquisite selection of gowns.

Montage 661-5328
3632 University
Houston, Texas 77005
- Montage is a charming little shop made up of three rooms filled with beautiful garments for the bride, including everything from lingerie to veils, hats, shoes and gowns.

DRESSING WITH STYLE

Storybook Weddings　　　　　　　　522-6801
River Oaks Center
2015 G West Gray
Houston, Texas 77019
- Storybook Weddings is a beautiful little shop which gives the bride-to-be much needed personal attention. They carry dresses for brides, bridesmaids, mothers of the brides and second time brides.

Mothers of the Bride and Groom

When looking for a dress keep in mind....

- Colors which compliment your skin tone (don't wear a mother of the bride pastel if it does not suit you)
- Silhouettes which compliment your figure
- Never purchase a dress that will not be able to worn again

Mothers of the Bride and Groom Wardrobe Choices

- Whether the wedding is formal or informal a short, tea length or floor length dress or suit is appropriate
- The mothers' ensembles should compliment each other in style, color and length

Bridesmaids Wardrobe Choices

Whether the wedding is formal or informal, a floor length, tea length, or short dress or suit is appropriate. If the bride wears a short dress, the bridesmaids should also wear short dresses. The more formal the wedding, the more opulent the fabric should be.

How to Have Happy and Beautiful Bridesmaids

Keep in mind when choosing bridesmaids dresses...

- Never force your bridesmaids to wear their hair a certain way.
- The dress color should compliment the bridesmaids' skin tone as well as the bride's.
- Choose a flattering dress style that will also compliment the lines of the bridal gown.
- Advise them on jewelry to wear. Simple pearl earrings and a pearl necklace look the most elegant.
- Keep the dress cost to a minimum unless the bride is able to absorb half the cost. The bridesmaids will never (even if the bride thinks they can) wear their dresses again.

Wardrobe Planning for Parties

The numerous parties a bride may need to look her best at include...

Bachelorette Party
Bar Shower
Bridesmaid's Luncheon
Engagement Party
Kitchen Shower
Lingerie Shower
Linen Shower
Mexican Buffet
Rehearsal Dinner
Tea

Before purchasing your party wardrobe ask yourself...
- Will I be able to wear this outfit again? If it is "costumey" or something no one will forget, don't buy it
- Will it make me look and feel special?

* Remember- It is always better to buy a few good quality pieces you can mix and match with than a lot of mediocre clothing.

The Honeymoon Wardrobe

A bride's trousseau was originally intended as the final grand gift from parents to their daughter. It was a complete wardrobe for the bride to use on her honeymoon and see her through the first year of marriage. Today the custom varies, but every bride usually purchases at least a few new outfits when planning her wedding.

Wardrobe Packing Tips

- Comfortable clothes which pack easily
- Clothes which mix and match
- Non-wrinkling fabrics
- Plenty of bras, socks and lingerie (who wants to spend time washing while on their honeymoon)
- A beautiful gown and robe set for the wedding night

Accessory Packing Tips

- Comfortable shoes
- One casual and one dressy purse
- One casual and one dressy belt
- Scarves and costume jewelry to change the look of outfits

IX

Wardrobe Building for College Girls

"Fashion comes and goes - style stays forever."
- *PATI TEIRNEY*
  LESLIE & CO.
  BUYER

The Basics of a College Girl's Wardrobe

Dressy Basics

One Suit • Neutral colored in a light-weight wool crepe or garbardine

Two Blazers	• Double-breasted navy or black • Single-breasted in flattering color
Two Skirts	• Slim skirt in light weight wool crepe in a neutral color • Sarong or pleated skirt
One Dress	• Black light weight wool crepe
One Blouse	• White or cream silk blouse
Two Pumps	• Black leather, suede or patent leather
One Purse	• Black leather good quality purse
Two Belts	• Lizard belt • Leather belt
Jewelry	• Pearl necklace • Pearl earrings

* It is best to keep valuables at home- take fine jewelry copies only.

Casual Basics

Shirts	• Set of six white Hanes t-shirts • Denim work shirt • White work shirt

Jackets	• Casual blazer • Jean jacket • Warm jacket to wear to school
Shorts	• Khaki • Denim • White • Black
Pants	• Jeans • Black leggings • Stirrup pants or jodhpurs
Shoes	• Keds or similar tennis shoes • Athletic tennis shoes • Loafers or other comfortable shoes for class • Slingback flats • Brown hiking boots • Western boots
Purses	• Brown or black purse for everyday • Totebag for class
Belts	• Lizard or alligator belt with silver buckle • Concho belt
Jewelry	• Gold loops • Sante Fe style jewelry in silver, turquoise and coral

* Remember, think quality not quantity.

DRESSING WITH STYLE

Dressing for Sorority Rush

BAYLOR

Open House - Nice dress or skirt outfit. (Two days in October)
Open House - Church clothes. (Two days after Chistmas break)
Skit Day - Slacks, skirts. Plan to be sitting on the floor.
Slide Show Day - Casual skirt or slacks outfit.
Pref Day - Dinner dress.

UNIVERSITY OF HOUSTON

Open House- Shorts or skirt outfit. Casual sundress. (Two days)
Invitational Parties - Luncheon or church styles.
Pref Night - Dinner or luncheon dress.

L.S.U.

First Party - Skirt or knit outfit. Casual dress but no shorts.
Second Party - Dress. Flats.
Third Party - Dressier dress than second day. Flats.
Acceptance Day- Church or luncheon dress.

UNIVERSITY OF MISSISSIPPI

Open House - Nice shorts outfit.
Coke Party - Casual dress. Flats.
Skit Party - Church outfit.
Pref Night - Cocktail dress.

UNIVERSITY OF NORTH TEXAS

Open House - Nice shorts outfit. Casual dress. Flats.
First Period - Dress or skirt outfit.
Second Period - Church or luncheon dress.

UNIVERSITY OF OKLAHOMA

Open House - Shorts or casual skirt outfit. Flats.
Seven Party Day - Skirt outfit or sundress. Flats.
Four Party Day - Luncheon dress.
Two Party Day - Dressier than Four Party Day but not cocktail.
Bid Day - Very casual shorts outfit.

SOUTHWEST TEXAS

Open Hall - Casual skirt or shorts outfit.
First Period - Luncheon or church dress.
Second Period - Casual sundress or skirt outfit.
Third Period - Cocktail dress.
Acceptance - Church or luncheon dress.

SOUTHWESTERN (After Christmas)

First Party - Slacks or jeans. Very casual.
Second Party - Luncheon or church dress.
Third Party - Cocktail dress.

DRESSING WITH STYLE

S.M.U. (After Christmas)

Open House - Casual dress or slacks. Flats.
Second Party - Casual dress or skirt but dressier than Open House.
Third Party - Luncheon or church dress.
Pref Night - Cocktail or dinner dress.

TEXAS TECH

Convocation - Very casual shorts outfit, knits.
First Period - Casual sundress, skirt or shorts outfit.
Second Period - Same as First Period.
Third Period - Luncheon or church styles.
Pref night - Semi-formal or dinner dress.
Bid Day - Shorts.

T.C.U.

First Period - Nice shorts outfit. (Two days)
Second Period - Casual skirt or sundress.
Third Period - Church or luncheon styles.
Pref Night - Dinner dress.
Bid Day - Nice skirt, shorts or sundress.

STEPHEN F. AUSTIN

First Round - Luncheon or church dress.
Second Round - Same as Round One.
Third Round - Same as Round One.
Pref Night - Cocktail or dressy Sunday dress.

TEXAS A & M

First Period - Casual shorts or skirt outfit.
Second Period - Dressier than First Period. No shorts.
Third Period - Nice dress or skirt outfit. Flats.
Fourth Period - Luncheon or church styles.
Pref Night - Cocktail dress.
Bid Day - Shorts or jeans.

VANDERBILT

House Tours - Casual sundress or nice shorts outfit. (September)
First Round - Nice skirt, pants or shorts outfit. (Two days)
Second Round Party - Same as First Round but a little dressier. (Two days)
Fourth Round Party - Cocktail dress.

UNIVERSITY OF TEXAS

Convocation - Casual shorts outfit.
• The look is very Santa Fe casual. No sorority girls are there. You see a mixture of jean shirts, khaki pants, Ralph Lauren lizard belts, Cole-Haan loafers, concho belts, pleated shorts, dressy t-shirts and Ralph Lauren scarves as belts. No dresses. Other convocations are immediatly after parties.

Open House - Skirt and top. Nice shorts outfit. (Two days)
• The parties are 30-minute long parties where you meet a lot of girls. The look you see includes dressy t-shirts, printed wrap skirts, concho belts, hurache sandals, brown woven

DRESSING WITH STYLE

slingbacks and belts. Linen shirts are popular but no linen shorts or skirts are worn because they get too wrinkled. No hose and few sundresses. Many of the girls change at noon so that they look and feel their best all day.

First Period - Nice skirt and blouse. Nice sundress or casual dress.
• The styles are a little dressier than Open House. You see nice shirts (not t-shirt styles), simplified Chanel looks, silk Ralph Lauren wrap skirts with shell blouses. Mostly blouses and skirts are worn. Dressier fabrics. Still silver jewelry.

Second Period - Church or Luncheon outfit.
• Nautical looks - Pleated skirts with double breasted blazers and white or pastel colored linen suits are popular. Nothing too "suity" or businesslike. Ralph Lauren scarves in hair.

Third Period - Dinner dress.
• No strapless, lace, sequins, ruffles, very high heels, French twists, tons of make-up or anything flashy. Silks, no linens. Stay with a 1 1/2 inch heel. The look is understated and classic. Jewelry worn includes pearl necklaces, pearl studs, pearl bracelets and gold jewelry. Hose are worn. This is pref night. The desired effect is pristine, understated class.

Bid Night: Dress or luncheon outfits.
• The atmosphere is cheery and lively with girls in bright colors and linen dresses, sundresses and luncheon outfits. Low heels. Pearls or silver jewelry.

* In order to give you a feel of exactly what the girls wear during Rush, I wrote a detailed accounting of dress during the University of Texas Rush with the help of an active. Be sure and check with Panhellenic and Rush Board members about the party schedule and dress codes because Rush rules are constantly in transition.

A College Girls' Favorite Designers

Ralph Lauren
Adrienne Vittadini
DKNY
Cole-Haan for shoes, especially in browns.

Stores to Shop at for Rush

Scott Wynne in Houston and Austin.
Polo Shop in Houston and Dallas.
Harold's in Houston, Dallas and Austin.
Leslie & Co. in Houston.
Grove Hill in San Antonio.
Beth Denius in Austin.

Lisa Galo, a Kappa Alpha Theta at the University of Texas described Rush dressing from an active's perspective, "During Rush, all the girls appear very sweet and innocent looking in their Ralph Lauren sarong skirted outfits. But once Rush is over, their true fashion personality comes out. You see more sophisticated looks such as blazers, leggings and mules."

The look is natural, clean and understated; nothing too

sophisticated. Basically you want to appear clean, cool and relaxed but Lisa suggested that, "You might want to do something a little bit different so people remember you but you don't want to over do it."

During the summer before Freshman year and at Rush dates the girls wear the same lines of clothes. Even when the Rush date is outside or at the lake, the look is pulled together. You see a lot of white Keds with push down white socks. Also, you don't see a lot of wild looks at parties before Rush.

X

CLOSET ORGANIZATION: FROM CHAOS TO CLEANLINESS

"Style is captured by ones individual look, an attitude - something that can't be bought, sold or copied. You've got it - or you don't."

- LINDA SEGAL
LINDA SEGAL FOR ASHLEY, INC.
PRESIDENT

consultant, the first place I begin with new clients is in the closet. Cleaning out a closet can be a most frustrating endeavor unless you follow a structured plan. After organizing many seemingly hopeless closets, I have devised this simple plan to follow.

The less time you spend deciding what to wear and getting dressed, the more time you will have for work and family. Also, you will save money shopping by knowing exactly what you need.

A Step- by- Step Organization Plan

<u>Step One</u> - Keep It Pile 1
   Separate each article of (trying on if needed) clothing, shoes and accessories into wearables in pile 1, maybes in pile 2 and toss its in pile 3.

<u>Step Two</u> - Maybes Pile 2
   Determine whether to keep the pieces in pile 2 by trying them on and asking yourself these questions:

- Can it be reconstructed?
- Does it mix and match in my wardrobe?
- When was the last time I wore it?
- Does it slenderize or add weight?
- Is it worth spending the money to have it altered?

* Put all "keep it" pieces in pile 1. If it's not worth it's once a year wear, toss it into Pile 3.

CLOSET ORGANIZATION

<u>Step Three</u> - Toss it Pile 3
   Donate all outdated and worn garments or take them to a re-sale shop. Cash earned from a re-sale shop over the years can add up to new purchases.

<u>Step Four</u> - Organize It
   Before putting anything back in your closet, take the following steps.

- Mix and match outfits, trying new combinations.
- Determine what key pieces are missing.
- Make a shopping list of your needs and wants.
- Make sure all garments fit properly, have updated hem lines and replace or sew buttons that are loose or missing. Also, make sure all shoe toes and heels are in perfect condition. If you don't fix them, you can't wear them.

Tips for an Organized Closet

- Hang garments from light to dark, left to right.
- Make sure all hangers are of uniform height and color. Throw out old yellowed, beat up or wire hangers.
- Fold all sweaters and knits and put them on a shelf, in drawers. Years of hanging will stretch them.
- Hang suits jackets and skirts separately. This gives you the opportunity to see more clearly how to mix and match pieces.
- Always hang garments and put accessories in the proper place on a daily basis.
- Check for spots, loose buttons and remove excess lint with an adhesive lint roller before hanging in your closet.

- Close all zippers and buttons.
- Leave space between clothes so they can air and so they will not crease one another.
- Always have seasonal clothes and shoes cleaned before storing away.

Keep the Following Items in a Drawer in Your Closet

- Helmac adhesive lint roller.
- Remington pill shaver for sweaters.
- Kiwi neutral self-shining shoe polish.
- Tana all-protector spray for leather and suede.
- Goddard's dry-clean spot remover.
- Old toothbrush.
- Suede brush.
- Safety pins.
- Box for extra buttons that have been included with new garments.

The following pages are for you to fill out while you organize your wardrobe. Don't forget to keep *Dressing with Style* with you in your purse so that you will always have a list of what you already have, what you really need and what you would like to have in your wardrobe.

Wardrobe Inventory & Plan

BLAZERS

Spring/Summer   Fall/Winter

In closet:

Needs:

Wants:

SUITS

      Spring/Summer   Fall/Winter

In closet:

Needs:

Wants:

BLOUSES

Spring/Summer   Fall/Winter

In closet:

Needs:

Wants:

SKIRTS

Spring/Summer	Fall/Winter

In closet:

Needs:

Wants:

PANTS

Spring/Summer	Fall/Winter

In closet:

Needs:

Wants:

SWEATERS

Spring/Summer   Fall/Winter

In closet:

Needs:

Wants:

DRESSES

Spring/Summer	Fall/Winter

In closet:

Needs:

Wants:

COCKTAIL & FORMAL DRESSES

Spring/Summer   Fall/Winter

In closet:

Needs:

Wants:

COCKTAIL SUITS

Spring/Summer   Fall/Winter

In closet:

Needs:

Wants:

JACKETS & COATS

      Spring/Summer   Fall/Winter

In closet:

Needs:

Wants:

SHIRTS

Spring/Summer	Fall/Winter

In closet:

Needs:

Wants:

SHORTS & LEGGINGS

Spring/Summer					Fall/Winter

In closet:

Needs:

Wants:

SWEATSUITS, EXERCISE WEAR, SWIMSUITS & COVERUPS

      Spring/Summer   Fall/Winter

In closet:

Needs:

Wants:

BELTS & SCARVES

Spring/Summer   Fall/Winter

In closet:

Needs:

Wants:

HANDBAGS & HATS

Spring/Summer   Fall/Winter

In closet:

Needs:

Wants:

SHOES

Spring/Summer   Fall/Winter

In closet:

Needs:

Wants:

JEWELRY

Spring/Summer	Fall/Winter

In closet:

Needs:

Wants:

NIGHTGOWNS, ROBES, HOSE/SOCKS & LINGERIE

Spring/Summer   Fall/Winter

In closet:

Needs:

Wants:

CLOSET ORGANIZATION NEEDS

( ) Hangers
( ) Rolling Rods
( ) Shoe Boxes
( ) Lingerie Separaters

NOTES:

Clothing Care and Maintenance

Cleaning and Storage Tips for Special Care Garments

Leather and Suede
- Clean only by a leather and suede specialist.
- Multiple-piece garments should be cleaned together.
- Wipe with a soft, damp cloth occasionally.
- Use an Artgum eraser for dirt spots.
- Never store in a plastic bag.

Velvet
- To clean, steam iron on the reverse side and lightly brush to raise the pile.
- Hang on padded hangers.

Cashmere
- Store folded in a plastic bag laying flat- do not hang.
- Use a clothes brush after pilling appears.
- Wash in cool water with mild soap flakes.

Silks
- Do not store in plastic bags or dry-cleaner bags.
- Drape cotton sheets or tissue paper over shoulders for long-term storage.

Shoe Care

- The same pair of shoes should not be worn two days in a row so that they can dry out.
- Keep cedar shoe trees in them to retain their shape.
- At the end of each season, check all shoes for scuff marks, worn heels and soles. Now is the time to get them fixed so that they will be ready for the next season.

CLOSET ORGANIZATION

Storage Tips

- Always clean clothes before storing.
- Never store clothes in plastic bags- it builds mildew and causes yellowing. If you must cover the garments, store them in cotton cloth cover so the fabric can breathe.
- Store furs in cool, dry place.

Jewelry care

Silver

- Clean regularly worn jewelry every two to three weeks.
- Rub the surface with a silver cloth.
- For detailed jewelry, dunk in liquid silver polish and wash with soapy lukewarm water. Then, buff with a chamois cloth.
- When using a brush only use one with soft bristles.

Gold

- Wash with lukewarm water and a little ammonia, then buff with a chamois cloth.
- Do not use a brush.

Jewelry With Set Stones

- Soak for fifteen minutes in warm, soapy water and them wipe with a soft cloth.
- Dry with a hair-dryer on low to dry water which may have seeped into the setting.
- Use ammonia and water then dry with a jewelry cloth to keep diamonds sparkling.

Stain Removal Guide

If treated correctly, most stains can be removed from washable fabrics at home. Always save care label and tags of every item of clothing to ensure proper care.

- First identify the stain and fabric type. Determine if the fabric is washable or bleachable, but remember the wrong pre-treatment can make a stain permanent.
- A spot on dry-cleanable fabric should be treated professionally.
- Never iron over a stain or expose the garment to heat or sunlight. This will set the stain permanently.
- Never chlorine bleach acrylics, silks, spandex or wools.
- Wash all washable fabrics after removing a stain.
- For liquid spills, blot excess liquid with an absorbent material. Do not apply pressure or the stain will be forced further into the material.
- For non-greasy stains on washable fabrics, flush with water or club soda.
- For greasy stains, douse with powder or chalk then brush off.
- Stains are divided into three categories:
    1. Greasy (butter, cream, lipstick, carbon bar)
    2. Non-greasy (black coffee, tea, sugar, alcohol, perspiration)
    3. Combination greasy/non-greasy (chocolate, ice cream, and sugar and fat mixtures)

CLOSET ORGANIZATION

The following supplies, if kept on hand at home, will prepare you to remove almost every stain.

- Absorbent materials - Clean white cloths, cotton, sponges. To absorb greasy stains: talcum powder, cornstarch or chalk.
- Rubbing alcohol - Always test fabric for color-fastness before using.
- Ammonia - Ammonium hydroxide or household ammonia.
- Brushes - Shoe polish brushes.
- Chlorine bleach - The most common stain remover. Never pour directly on stain - always dilute.
- Detergent - Use a mild, pure liquid dishwashing or fabric detergent, such as Ivory.
- Drycleaning solvent - Many commercial brands are available in drug stores.
- Glycerine - Removes many stains, works well on ballpoint ink.
- Hydrogen peroxide - Use the mild kind sold as an antiseptic.
- Salt - Any household table salt.
- Vinegar - White distilled vinegar.

COMMON STAINS
&
How to Remove Them from Washable Fabrics

BLEACHABLE FABRICS
(White and Colorfast cottons, linens, polyester, acrylic, triacetate, nylon, rayon, permanent press.)

NON-BLEACHABLE FABRICS
(Wool, silk, spandex, non-colorfast items, some fabric finishes.)

ALCOHOLIC BEVERAGES

Sponge stain immediatly with cold water. Rub detergent into any remaining stain while still wet. Wash in hot water using chlorine bleach.

Sponge with cold water, then vinegar. Rinse well. If stain remains, rub detergent into stain. Rinse and wash according to fabric instructions. No bleach.

BLOOD

Soak in cold water for 1/2 hour. If stain remains, rub in detergent and rinse. If detergent doesn't work, mix 1 tablespoon of ammonia with 1 cup water, and rub into stain. Rinse very well before washing with chlorine bleach.

Follow same steps, but use hydrogen peroxide instead of ammonia. Rinse and wash according to fabric instructions. No bleach.

COFFEE, TEA

Black coffee and tea stains will usually be removed by simple washing. Sponge stain with cleaning fluid if cream used. Wash in hot water using chlorine bleach.

Soak in cold water, rub detergent into stain. Rinse and dry. If cream leaves grease stain, sponge with cleaning fluid. Rinse and wash according to fabric instructions.

COSMETICS

Dampen stain with detergent until outline of stain is gone. Rinse well. Wash in hot water using chlorine bleach.

Follow same steps. Rinse and wash according to fabric instructions. No bleach.

FINGERNAIL POLISH

Sponge white cotton fabric with nail polish remover. All other fabrics use amyl acetate (banana oil). Wash, repeat if necessary.

Follow same steps. Rinse and wash according to fabric instructions. No bleach.

CLOSET ORGANIZATION

BLEACHABLE FABRICS	NON-BLEACHABLE FABRICS
(White and Colorfast cottons, linens, polyester, acrylic, triacetate, nylon, rayon, permanent press.)	(Wool, silk, spandex, non-colorfast items, some fabric finishes.)

GREASE AND OIL

On a fresh stain, rub in an absorbent powder (talcum) and brush off. If the grease has penetrated the fabric, rub detergent into dampened stain. Wash in hot water with chlorine bleach. If that doesn't work, sponge with drycleaning fluid. Rinse and wash again.

Follow same steps. Rinse and wash according to fabric instructions. No bleach.

INK (BALLPOINT)

Sponge stain with rubbing alcohol or spray with hair spray until wet. Rinse. Then rub detergent into stained area and wash. Alternate method: Rub glycerine into stain then wash.

Follow same steps. Rinse and wash according to fabric instructions. No bleach.

PERSPIRATION

Rub detergent into dampened stain. Wash in hot water using chlorine bleach. If fabric is discolored: treat new stains with ammonia and old stains with vinegar. Rinse and wash.

Follow same steps. Rinse and wash according to fabric instructions. No bleach.

RED WINE

Sprinkle immediatly with salt. Salt will absorb the red color and brush off. As soon as possible, soak in cold water. Rub detergent into any remaining stain. Wash in hot water using chlorine

Sprinkle with salt and brush off. Sponge with cold water. Then vinegar. Rinse. If stain remains, rub detergent into stain. Rinse and wash. No bleach.

XI

Houston Beauty and Fashion Experts

"Style is determined by one's own ability to visually communicate. Communication that is visual and verbal set a style president for each one's personality. Therefore communicating accurately gets us what we want."

- HEIDI SCHULZE
STARMAKER AT URBAN RETREAT
MAKE-UP ARTIST

Bene Fit 523-3223
2428 Times Blvd.
Houston, Texas 77005
- Bene Fit is an innovative boutique carrying make-up and skin care products. Elixirs of plants, herbs, vitamins and minerals make up their bio-botanical treatment and color line.

DRESSING WITH STYLE

Patti Bruni 289-5100
Personal Trainer
Kevin Bozant 859-1742
Fitness Consultant & Tae Kwando Instructer
- Personal training service providing today's state-of-the-art workouts with an emphasis on overall conditioning.

Tina Fondren 974-0370
Fashion & Design Consultant
- Tina Fondren is Fashion & Design Consultant specializing in wardrobe analysis, closet analysis, personal shopping and fashion design.

Jacques Dessange 960-1010
1800 Post Oak Blvd., Suite 192
Houston, Texas 77056
- French owners Claudie and Reno Jasper have brought French style to Houston with their beautiful salon and fabulous hair stylists, colorists and manicurists.

A Perfect Fit by Irene 266-0269
5901 Westheimer, Suite J
Houston, Texas 77057
- Irene D' Attilio's shop combines excellent alterations with impeccable customer service.

Harry's Shoes & Boots 622-8315
4214 San Felipe
Houston, Texas 77027
- Harry Stefanides who learned his trade in Athens, Greece is the only person in Houston with the skills to properly repair or dye damaged shoes, purses and belts.

HOUSTON BEAUTY AND FASHION EXPERTS

Programme Martin 961-1130
3601 West Alabama
Houston, Texas 77027
- Programme Martin produces a state-of-the-art closet system designed to increase closet capacity and performance. It is the most organized and beautiful closet system available in Houston.

Sensia Studio 627-0070
1711 Post Oak Blvd.
Houston, Texas 77056
- The excellent location, intimacy of the salon and oustanding services makes Sensia Studio an excellent choice for hair styling, manicures and make-up lessons from well- known Houston make-up artist Cynthia Christ.

Jenifer of Australia 520-1070
2437½ University
Houston, Texas 77077
- Natural light and an exotic setting makes Jenifer of Australia a truly unique experience. She offers facials, full body massage, manicures and pedicures. Jenifer received her training in Australia, France and Austria.

Urban Retreat 523-2300
2329 San Felipe
Houston, Texas 77019

- From their courteous staff to the sound of trickling water the Urban Retreat is truly like going into a luxurious retreat. This full service salon offers a wide range of services including hair color and cuts, electrolysis, reflexology, massages, hydrotherapy treatments, facials, manicures, pedicures and even has it's own boutique. Extra amenities include private rooms, complimentary valet parking and an international staff. Heidi Schulze is their nationally known make-up artist who has worked her make-up magic on many celebrities including Jane Seymour, Cindy Crawford and Priscilla Presley. Heidi is available for make-up lessons and applications for special events, photographic sessions and weddings.

XII

The Best Shopping in Houston: A Retail Directory

"Style is an individual's personal interpretation of classic and contemporary fashion that gives her a recognizable 'signature,' a look all her own - i.e. Greek style, Roman style, Ms. style!"

- SARAH S. BOYD
Ms.
OWNER

- A -

Accessory Lady 552-0128
Galleria II
Houston, Texas 77056
- A great store to find trendy and classic inexpensive purses, scarves, hats and costume jewelry. They always stock those hard to find earring pads.

Ann Taylor 627-3722
Galleria II
Houston, Texas 77056
- Ann Taylor carries resonably price lines such as Andrea Jovine, Tahari and their private label line, Ann Taylor.

Armani Exchange 850-1995
Galleria II
Houston, Texas 77056
- Armani Exchange carries solely Giorgio Armani's secondary line, Armani Jeans. The look of the Italian designer's line is sophisticated, casual sportswear.

- B -

Banana Republic 621-4451
Galleria I
Houston, Texas 77056
- A great place for inexpensive, quality basics such as denim shirts, khaki shorts and woven belts.

Barneys New York 622-3636
Galleria I
Houston, Texas 77056
- Barneys offers some of the most innovative merchandise in Houston. They carry many designers exclusive to Houston and offer a private label line which is ideal for professional women. In the private label line you may choose between a wide selection of silhouettes and fabrics. They offer complimentary alterations.

BBI 942-7565
Shepard Square
2055 Westheimer
Houston, Texas 77098
- BBI is a great boutique selling reasonably priced lines not found at other stores such as Michael Stars, Patricia Jones and Bonnie Strauss.

Bottega Veneta 626-5611
Galleria I
Houston, Texas 77056
- Bottega Veneta carries gorgeous leather accessories including belts and purses that last for years.

- C -

Carrano 961-3133
Galleria II
Houston, Texas 77056
- Carrano carries beautiful Italian made shoes under the Maraolo label.

Cignal 622-7652
Galleria I
Houston, Texas 77056
- A fabulous place to find trendy clothes and accessories to update your wardrobe.

Classic Handbags 840-1999
4252 Richmond Ave.
Houston, Texas 77027
- Classic handbags carries the best quality and selection of designer look-a-like handbags and jewelry in Houston.

Cotton Club 522-9101
Cotton Club Sport 522-9101
River Oaks Center
1956- A West Gray
Houston, Texas 77019
- The Cotton Club is known for their eclectic mix of casual clothing lines such as Ghost and Sue Wong.

- D -

Dance Centre 522-0031
River Oaks Center
2041 West Gray
Houston, Texas 77019
- A small boutique which carries the most unique and newest exercise clothing and active sportswear lines in Houston.

Deborah Brown Designs 467-5729
1000 Cambell Rd. #208-682
Houston, Texas 77057
- Deborah Brown Designs offers high quality custom leather and suede apparel. You may choose between many styles and colors. By appointment only.

Dillard's 622-1200
4925 Westheimer
Houston, Texas 77056
- The newly renovated Dillard's is absolutely beautiful. They now carry a great selection of diffusion lines including Emanuel, MM by Krizia and DKNY.

Dimensions 780-8564
7619 Westheimer
Houston, Texas 77063
- Dimensions carries current designer merchandise such as Adrienne Vittadini, Andrea Jovine and Bill Blass dresses at about 20% below retail prices.

Doreen's Refinery 629-5818
4745 Westheimer
Houston, Texas 77027
- Doreen's Refinery is the best re-sale shop in Houston because not only is it merchandised well, but they only accept spotless, up-to-date clothing and accesssories.

- E -

Ella Pryor 521-2235
2992 Kirby
Houston, Texas 77098
- Ella Pryor originated years ago in Pasedena and is now a beautiful boutique which carries casual and dressy designer lines such as Michael Kors, Todd Oldham, Randy Kemper and A.B.S. of California.

Episode 621-4703
Galleria II
Houston, Texas 77056
- Episode's beautiful line of clothes strongly resembles those by Calvin Klein and Giorgio Armani at much better prices. All of the color groups mix and match and are made of fine quality fabrics. A great store to find dressy basics and a favorite of mine to take professional clients to.

Etui 627-2212
3433 West Alabama
Houston, Texas 77027
- Etui is a service orientated boutique carrying lines such as Votre Nom of Paris, Nicole Miller and Elleanor Brenner. They keep their clients informed on fashion trends through shows, workshops and newsletters.

THE BEST SHOPPING IN HOUSTON

Eye Elegance 622-4411
The Pavilion
1800 Post Oak Boulevard
Houston, Texas 77056
- Eye Elegance not only offers great customer service but has an excellent selection of designer frames including Gianfranco Ferre, Christian Lacroix, Cartier and Persol.

Events 520-5700
River Oaks Shopping Center
1966 West Grey
Houston, Texas 77019
- Events has a small area carrying unique jewelry and handbags by designers such as Leslie Block, Lazaro and Deanna Hamro.

- F -

Fendi 961-1111
Galleria I
Houston, Texas 77056
- Fendi is the Italian leather goods company famous for their luxurious line of purses, luggage, clothing and watches.

Fogal 621-8658
Galleria I
Houston, Texas 77056
- Fogal carries the finest and most expensive hosiery in the world. If you ever need a special color of hose they carry a wide range of new and different colors.

- G -

Gallery of Fabrics 621-1731
3641 Westheimer
Houston, Texas 77027
- The Gallery of Fabrics stocks the most beautiful designer, European and bridal fabrics. Their courteous salespeople will help you with fabric, button and pattern selections.

The Gap 626-8191
Galleria I
Houston, Texas 77056
4030 Westheimer 877-1271
Houston, Texas 77027
6225 Kirby Drive 942-7061
Houston, Texas 77005
1200 McKinney at The Park 658-1820
Houston, Texas 77010
- The Gap is famous for their all-American sportswear basics such as jeans, t-shirts and khaki pants.

Gianni Versace 623-8220
Galleria I
Houston, Texas 77056
- The Italian designer Versace designs for the fashion forward woman who is not afraid of wild patterns and color.

Guess 621-2729
Galleria II
Houston, Texas 77056
- Guess carries trendy jeans and sportswear in the newest styles of the season.

Gucci 961-0778
Galleria II
Houston, Texas 77056
- The world famous Gucci line has updated their image and now offers classic handbags, shoes, belts, jewelry and clothing for women of all ages.

- H -

Harold Powell 840-7681
4010 Westheimer
Houston, Texas 77027
- Harold Powell, known by the name Harold's in Dallas, carries Ralph Lauren, Harold's private label line, Breeches and Joan and David shoes.

Harriet Hart 523-3700
2501 River Oaks Blvd.
Houston, Texas 77019
- Harriet Hart's store carries great accessories as well as designers such as Nolan Miller, Liancarlo, Bill Blass and Randy Kemper.

The Hat Store 780-2480
5587 Richmond
Houston, Texas 77056
- The Hat Store definitely has the best western and hunting hat selection in Houston. They also carry hat bands, belts, buckles and bola ties.

Hermes 623-2177
The Pavilion
1800 Post Oak Boulevard
Houston, Texas 77056
- Hermes carries their line of exquisite line of jewelry, clothing, handbags and scarves. Hermes originated in Paris and is a favorite of all French women.

The Houstonian Sports Shop 680-2626
The Houstonian Club
111 North Post Oak Lane
Houston, Texas 77024
- The Houstonian Sports Shop carries a fabulous selection of workout clothes, running clothes, swimsuits and casual wear.

- J -

Joan and David 840-7516
Galleria I
Houston, Texas 77056
- Joan and David carries their line of classic leather shoes and belts.

Joseph 623-8034
Highland Village
3920 Westheimer
Houston, Texas 77027
- Joseph is the best freestanding shoe store in Houston carrying lines such as Ferragamo, Stuart Weitzman and a private label line. They also carry beautiful purses and costume jewelry.

J•S Collections 529-5333
2411 Rice Blvd.
Houston, Texas 77005
- Thalian, Kathryn Dianos and Mancuso•Witkewicz are just a few of the young up-beat American designers sold at this great boutique.

Just Add Water 961-3891
Galleria II
Houston, Texas 77056
- Just Add Water offers a wide selection of the newest swimwear and cover-ups.

- K -

Katia 621-4246
5638 Westheimer
Houston, Texas 77056
- Katia is a fabulous boutique mostly known by word of mouth. They carry many of the newest designer lines from Los Angeles and New York. It is a great store to find unique sportswear such as stretch basics from British designer Liza Bruce.

Kenneth Jay Lane 622-4048
Galleria I
Houston, Texas 77056
- Kenneth Jay Lane is world famous for his costume jewelry modeled after fine jewelry. The triple strand pearl necklace Barbara Bush wears is by him.

- L -

Laurel 622-2001
Crisca
1800 Post Oak Boulevard
Houston, Texas 77056
- Laurel and Crisca are two adjacent stores carrying exclusively Laurel and Crisca which are divisions of Escada. The lines are classic in cut and color.

Leonard Rutan 524-9980
2710 Kirby Drive
Houston, Texas 77098
- Leonard Rutan stocks wonderful dresses and suit lines including CH by Carolina Herrera, Ann Lawrence and Oscar de la Renta Studio at his newly expanded boutique.

Leslie & Company 960-9113
1749 Post Oak Boulevard
Houston, Texas 77056
- Leslie & Company carries updated traditional clothing lines such as Barry Bricken, Breeches and Ralph Lauren as well as fabulous belts, jewelry and scarves. They offer complimentary alterations for the life of the garment.

The Limited 961-5301
Galleria II
Houston, Texas 77056
- The Limited is a great place to find inexpensive, everyday basics such as skirts, sweaters and leggings.

Loehmann's 777-0164
7455 Southwest Freeway
Houston, Texas 77074
- Loehmann's is the largest discount store in Houston which sells designer merchandise. Designers such as Karl Lagerfeld and Moschino can be found in the Back Room. Expect labels to be torn out but the designer name is often on the tags.

Louis Vuitton 960-0708
Galleria II
Houston, Texas 77056
- The world renowned leather goods company, Louis Vuitton, carries a wide range of handbags, leather accessories and luggage. They now manufacture beautiful products without the Louis Vuitton initials.

- M -

Macy's 968-1985
Galleria III
2727 Sage Road
Houston, Texas 77056
- The department store Macys carries everything from low to high end designers. Their petite department is the best in Houston.

Mariquita Masterson 522-6774
2138 Welch
Houston, Texas 77019
- Mariquita Masterson's design studio carries her unique hand-made glass jewelry. The casual atmosphere is ideal

for just browsing or bringing in an outfit to find matching jewelry. You may choose from different colors of glass and shapes to design your own look. Their beautiful jewelry is truly couture costume jewelry and can be worn with anything from a ball gown to jeans.

Mark Cross 626-4729
Galleria I
Houston, Texas 77056
- Mark Cross carries luxurious leather desk accessories purses and luggage. They offer a lifetime warranty on all of their luggage.

Marshall Fields 968-7222
Between Galleria II & III
Houston, Texas 77056
- Marshall Fields is an upscale department store. They have a great Juniors area and a large in-store DKNY boutique.

Max Lang 960-8845
Highland Village
4020 Westheimer
Houston, Texas 77027
- Max Lang carries the most beautiful selection of hand crafted exotic belts, sterling silver buckles and accessories worn by many well-known celebrities. You may bring in your own skins.

Mr. Goodbye's 523-7474
Artigiani Center
3423-A South Shepard Drive
Houston, Texas 77019

- Mr. Goodbye's is a fun and eclectic boutique carrying lines not usually seen at other stores and mostly only known by word of mouth.

Ms. 527-0113
River Oaks Center
2047 West Gray
Houston, Texas 77019
- Ms. is a wonderful boutique combining excellent personal service with traditional lines such as Anne Klein II, Kors and Ralph Lauren.

- N -

Neiman Marcus 621-7100
Galleria I
2600 Post Oak Boulevard
Houston, Texas 77056
10615 Town and Country Way 984-2100
Houston, Texas 77024
- Neiman Marcus is the most upscale department store in Houston carrying established designers as well as new up and coming designers in easy to shop in-store boutique settings. Their bi-annual Last Call is the best designer sale shopping in Houston with merchandise marked at up to 70% off.

North Beach Leather 629-5880
Galleria I
Houston, Texas 77056
- Michael Hoban designs the fashionable leather clothing for

North Beach Leather. Not only does North Beach Leather carry wild designs often worn by celebrities but also is the best place to find quality leather basics.

- O -

Optica 621-4225
Galleria II
Houston, Texas 77056
- Optica carries suglasses and prescription eyeglasses by designers such as Alain Mikli, Persol, Oliver Peeples and Jean Paul Gaultier.

Optique
4380 Westheimer at Midlane 626-3937
Houston, Texas 77027
- Optique offers a personalized approach to eyewear by providing optometry services and the latest designer sun glasses in styles by designers such as Paloma Picasso and Giorgio Armani.

Oshman's 622-4940
2131 South Post Oak Boulevard
Houston, Texas 77056
- For tennis, working out, skiing, hunting or just buying tennis shoes, Oshman's can take care of all of your sports clothing under one roof.

- P -

Patricia's 522-5740
2801 Bammel Lane
Houston, Texas 77098

- Patricia's is Houston's best evening rental boutique. They carry lines such as Victor Costa, A.J. Bari, Bob Mackie and Oscar de la Renta. At the end of each season the gowns are sold at or below cost price.

Polo Ralph Lauren 850-9330
Galleria III
Houston, Texas 77056
- If you want classic American clothing, Ralph Lauren's designs are always in style and made of the highest quality fabrics. Their shoes and accessories are equally outstanding.

Prestige Creation 960-0593
The Pavilion
1800 Post Oak Blvd.
Houston, Texas 77056
- Claudie Jasper, the Parisian owner of Jacques Dessange travels to Paris to find the newest Parisian designer lines that offer great French style at reasonable French prices.

- R -

R. J. Bootmaker 682-1650
3321 Ella Blvd.
Houston, Texas 77018
- Rocky Caroll's custom made boots are famous in Texas and now all over the U. S. as his boots are seen on many well known people including former President George Bush, Elizabeth Taylor and Suzanne Somers.

- S -

Sacha London 961-5246
Galleria II
Houston, Texas 77056
- Sacha London carries trendy reasonably priced shoes for the fashion forward shopper.

Saks Fifth Avenue 627-0500
1800 Post Oak Boulevard
Houston, Texas 77056
- The department store Saks Fifth Avenue is the anchor store of the Pavilion Center. Their couture department hosts many designer trunk shows throughout the year.

Silverlust 520-5440
1338-C Westheimer
Houston, Texas 77006
- Silverlust carries fabulous unique sterling silver and some gold jewelry. Their jewelry comes from all over the world and they can even custom design pieces for you. Their reasonably priced jewelry is an affordable way to update your wardrobe.

Southern Fabrics 626-5511
Galleria I
Houston, Texas 77056
- Southern fabrics is the only fabric store located within the Galleria. Their fabrics include everything from inexpensive cotton fabrics to imported laces.

THE BEST SHOPPING IN HOUSTON

- T -

Tootsies 629-9990
4045 Westheimer
Houston, Texas 77027
- The Houston based Tootsies is known for their upscale trendy merchandise and designer clothing such as Armani, Donna Karan, Givenchy and Calvin Klein. They also carry fabulous purses and jewelry.

Tootsies Dress Collection 439-0076
Galleria I
Houston, Texas 77056
- Bob Mackie Boutique, Liancarlo, Stanley Platos/Martin Ross, Andrea Jovine and Kathryn Dianos are just a few of the outstanding dress designers found at Tootsies Dress Collection.

Turquoise Lady 627-0973
Galleria I
Houston, Texas 77056
- If you are not planning to go to New Mexico anytime soon, you can find the most beautiful Indian jewelry and concho belts in Houston at the Turquoise Lady.

- V -

Versus 626-2107
Galleria I
Houston, Texas 77056
- Versus carries Italian designer, Gianni Versace's secondary line Versus and Istante. His colorful clothes are for the fashion forward shopper.

Victoria's Secret   622-8007
Galleria II
Houston, Texas 77056
- The Victoria's Secret line of beautiful lingerie includes everything from nightshirts to camisoles at reasonable prices.

Vikki   266-5252
6372 Richmond
Houston, Texas 77057
- Vikki's boutique is a small store offering excellent customer service and often holds trunk shows. They carry casual lines such as Votre Nom of Paris and their private label line, Vikki.

- Y -

Ylang Ylang   621-2015
Galleria III
Houston, Texas 77056
- Ylang Ylang offers unique, fun costume jewelry at reasonable prices.

- Z -

Zarina's   520-1883
2366-C Rice Boulevard
Houston, Texas 77005
- Zarina's small shop in West University carries designer merchandise up to 75% off retail prices. The lines they carry include Ungaro, Theirry Mugler and Escada.

GLOSSARY

- A -

Acrylic - Synthetic fibers used as a substitute for wool.

- B -

Bridal trousseau - The bride's trousseau was a complete wardrobe for the bride to use on her honeymoon and see her through her first year of marriage. It was originally intended as the final grand gift from parents to their daughter.

Bustier - It was originally an underwear garment based on a bra and camisole. Today bustiers are mostly worn for evening attire.

- C -

Chemise - A simple dress which is usually collarless, sleeveless and has no seams at the waist.

Cost Per Wearing - The C.P.W. is taking the price of a garment or accessory and dividing by the number of times it will probably be worn.

Couture - Couture is an abbreviation for haute couture. Haute couture is made-to-order, originally created garments. The term couture now also means limited editions of clothing.

- D -

Designer collections - American and European designers show a Fall/Winter, Spring and sometimes Resort or Summer collections every year on the fashion runways of New York, Los Angeles, Paris, Milan and London.

Diffusion lines - Designer lines which are more affordable and often more casual than their signature line. They are also called secondary lines.

Dolman sleeve - A sleeve extending from the bodice of a dress, blouse or jacket which has a deep wide armhole that tapers at the wrist.

- F -

French cuff - A cuff on the sleeve of a garment which folds over and has an opening for cuff links.

- G -

Garment codes - The RN or WPL number of a certain designer listed on the care label of a garment.

- I -

Investment dressing - The theory of dressing says that it is better to buy fewer good quality clothing than an excess of lower quality clothing.

-K-

Knockoff designers - Once the designer collections have been shown in Europe, many designers and fashion companies design garments which strongly resemble those by a certain couture designer.

-M-

Mules - Shoes similar to house slippers in that they do not have construction around the ankle. The heel height can range from flat to very high.

-P-

Pareo - A piece of fabric often hand dyed in Hawaii or the Caribbean which can be used as a scarf or a beach coverup tied around the body.

Private label line - A line of clothing or accessories a store produces in the state or abroad which is sold exclusively in that store.

-S-

Secondary line - See diffusion line.

Signature line - The primary line of a designer.

-T-

Trunk show - Trunk shows are held when clothing line's representative brings the designer's upcoming collection to a store.

INDEX

accessories 55, 65, 66, 67
   scarves 67, 130

boutiques 17
brides 69
   bridesmaids 74
   gown 70
   honeymoon wardrobe 76
   Houston bridal stores 72
   mothers of the bride and groom 74
   parties 75
   second wedding 70
   wardrobe checklist 71

catalogs 18
   shopping resources 19, 20
Chanel, Coco 12, 63
closet organization 87
   wardrobe inventory and plan 91
clothing care and maintenance 110
   cleaning and storage tips 110
   jewelry care 111
   shoe care 110
   stain removal guide 112
college girls 77
   dressing for Sorority Rush 80
   favorite designers 85
   stores 85
   wardrobe basics 77
colors 26
Cost Per Wearing 43

department stores 16
designers 31
   American 31
   British 35
   diffusion lines 38
   French 33
   German 36
   Italian 34
   size chart 37
   Japanese 36
diffusion lines 37

evening dressing 60
   classics 61
   little black dress 63

fabric 27
   lycra 28
   wool 27
   wool/silk 27
fashion signature 63
   figure types 24
   boyish 25
   full 26
   pear 25
   petite 24
French women 12, 67, 130

garment codes 47

Houston beauty and fashion experts 117
Houston bridal stores 72
Houston retail directory 121
Houston vintage stores 50

investment dressing 41, 42, 43, 44

knockoff designers 66

magazines 28
   Allure 28
   Bazaar 28
   Elle 28
   Vogue 29
   W. 29
   WWD 29
newspapers 29
   Houston Chronicle 29

NOTES

basics I lack

Simple blk dress

pants - wool (light weight)

winter ankle boots

bathing suits (2)

walking sneakers
aerobic sneakers

Doreens Refinery 629-5818
4745 Westheimer
Marguita Masterson 522-6774
2130 Welch (costume jewelry)

A Perfect fit by Irene (Irene D'Attilo) 5901 Westheimer
266-0269

N-M call to find out when
last call starts
Jan 16 (?)

Jan 2 ? Saks Designer Dress Sale
Talbots sale Jan 1
Jan Cotton Club Winter sale

DRESSING WITH STYLE

Houston Post 29

Popcorn, Faith 10
private label lines 40

Reagan, Nancy 64

sales 45
    strategies for 46
    calendar 48
secondary lines 38
silhouettes 24
signature lines 38
specialty stores 17

television programs 29
    Style With Elsa Klensch 29
travel wardrobe 57, 76
    basics 57, 58
    packing tips 58
trunk shows 17

vintage clothing stores 50
Vreeland, Diana 64
wardrobe 53, 69, 77
    basics for college girls 77
    bridal 69
    dressing for Sorority Rush 80
    evening 60
    foundation for a women 54
    inventory and plan 91
    travel 57, 76
Williamson, Marianne 11
Wintour, Anna 37

Tina Fondren
Fashion & Design Consultant

Tina Fondren, Houston's leading Fashion and Design Consultant, works with a diverse range of clients including professionals, charity fund-raisers and retail establishments such as the Galleria and Tootsies. Educated in fashion design and merchandising at the Otis Parsons School of Design and the University of Texas at Austin, Tina began her professional career as a personal shopper for Neiman Marcus. Her extensive background in the retail industry includes working with the Galleria, Saks Fifth Avenue, the Cotton Club and Seventeen Magazine. As associate editor of Houston Woman Magazine, Tina wrote the fashion column, "Fashion Workshop." Tina is a board member and charter member of the Association of Image Consultants International, Houston Chapter. She is fluent in Spanish and dresses Houston's best-dressed women. Her services include wardrobe analysis, closet organization, personal shopping and fashion design.

DESCRIPTION OF SERVICES

Wardrobe Analysis and Closet Analysis. An at home closet evaluation covering closet organization, designer profile, color analysis, figure type profile, mixing and matching techniques, alterations evaluation and planned shopping lists.

Personal Shopping. Personal shopping excursions with or without client. Shop certain stores according to budget, lifestyle and personal style while teaching clients how to effectively and value-consciously shop.

Fashion Design. Utilizing her education from the Otis Parsons School of Design and the University of Texas, Tina designs made-to-order cocktail and luncheon clothing.

YES! *I'm interested in your book/services.*

Name _____

Title _____

Company/Organization _____

_____

Address _____

City/State _____

Zip code _____

Phone _____

Please send *Dressing with Style - A Woman's Guide to Organizing Your Wardrobe & Shopping in Houston.*

_____ Copies @ $16.25 including shipping and handling.
Enclosed is my check or money order for $ _____ .
Please allow two to four weeks for delivery.

Tina Fondren
Fashion & Design Consultant
5251 Westheimer, Suite 320
Houston, Texas 77056-1562
713-974-0370

DRESSING WITH STYLE

NOTES

DRESSING WITH STYLE

NOTES

DRESSING WITH STYLE

NOTES

DRESSING WITH STYLE

NOTES

DRESSING WITH STYLE

NOTES

DRESSING WITH STYLE